HOW TO DO IT!

No matter what it is, the important question always is: "How to do it?"

The mind has many marvelous powers—far more than you have ever dreamed of—and humanity has barely begun the wonderful evolutionary journey that will let us tap into them all at will. We grow in our abilities as we do things.

There are many wonderful things you can do. As you do them, you learn more about the innate qualities of mind and spirit, and as you exercise these inner abilities, they will grow in strength—*as will your vision of your mental and spiritual potential.*

In learning to *See and Read the Aura*, or making a *Love Charm*, or using a *Magic Mirror*, or many other strange and wonderful things, you are extending—just a little bit—the tremendous gift that lies within, the Life Force itself.

We are born that we may grow, and not to use this gift—not to grow in your perception and understanding of it—is to turn away from the gifts of Life, of Love, of Beauty, of Happiness that are the very reason for Creation.

Learning how to do these things is to open psychic windows to New Worlds of Mind & Spirit. Actually doing these things is to enter into New Worlds. Each of these things that we do is a step forward in accepting responsibility for the worlds that you can shape and influence.

Simple, easy to follow, yet so very rewarding. Following these step-by-step instructions can start you upon high adventure. Gain control over the world around you, and step into *New Worlds of Mind & Spirit.*

About the Author

Ted Andrews is a full-time author, student and teacher in the metaphysical and spiritual fields. He conducts seminars, symposiums, and workshops and lectures throughout the country on many facets of ancient mysticism. Ted works with past-life analysis, auric interpretation, numerology, the tarot and the qabala as methods of developing and enhancing inner potential. He is a clairvoyant and a certified spiritualist medium.

Ted is also active in the healing field. He is certified in basic hypnosis and acupressure and is involved in the study and use of herbs. He is a contributing author to various metaphysical magazines with articles published on such subjects as "Occult Christianity," "Working With Our Angelic Brethren," and "Metaphysical Mirrors in Our Lives."

To Write to the Author

We cannot guarantee that every letter written to the author can be answered, but all will be forwarded. Both the author and the publisher appreciate hearing from readers, learning of your enjoyment and benefit from this book. Llewellyn also publishes a bi-monthly news magazine with news and reviews of practical esoteric studies and articles helpful to the student, and some readers' questions and comments to the author may be answered through this magazine's columns if permission to do so is included in the original letter. The author sometimes participates in seminars and workshops, and dates and places are announced in *The Llewellyn New Times*. To write to the author, or to ask a question, write to:

Ted Andrews
c/o The Llewellyn New Times
P.O. Box 64383-013, St. Paul, MN 55164-0383, U.S.A.
Please enclose a self–addressed, stamped envelope for reply, or $1.00 to cover costs.

How to See and Read the Aura

Ted Andrews

1992
Llewellyn Publications
St. Paul, Minnesota 55164–0383

FIRST EDITION
Second Printing, 1992

Cover photo by Michael Yencho
Illustrations by Christopher Wells

Library of Congress Cataloging-in-Publication Data
Andrews, Ted, 1952—
  How to see and read the aura/Ted Andrews—
    p.   cm. — (Llewellyn's how to series)
  Includes bibliographical references.
  ISBN 0–875420–013–3
    1. Aura.   I. Title.   II. Series
  BF1389.A8A55 1991
  133.8—dx20
                                            90–28285
                                               CIP

Llewellyn Publications
A Division of Llewellyn Worldwide, Ltd.
P.O. Box 64383, St. Paul, MN 55164-0383

Dedication

To Kathy and the Girls

CONTENTS

1

What Is the Aura?

Everyone has an aura. Everyone has already seen or experienced the auric fields of others. The problem is that most people ignore the experience or chalk it up to something that it is not.

Mystics from all parts of the world speak of seeing lights around people's heads, but you do not have to be a mystic to see the aura. Anyone can learn to see and experience the aura more effectively. There is nothing magical about the process. It involves recognizing it for what it is and not ignoring the experience. It simply involves a little understanding, time, practice and perseverance. On page 3 is a questionnaire about the aura. If you can answer yes to one or more of the questions, you have already experienced the energy of the aura.

Children are very good at seeing and experiencing the aura. Those experiences are often translated into their drawings. Around the figures, they will shade in unusual and different colors. These colors often reflect the subtle energies they have observed around what they are drawing.

Too frequently such pictures are greeted with "Why is the sky purple around Mommy?", "Why is the cat green and pink?" or "Why did you make your brother blue?" It is not that the cat is green and pink or that the brother is blue. It is simply that the child has experienced these auric colors and then uses the colors of the crayons to help express what was seen. Unfortunately, such comments serve only to help shut down these subtle perceptions and awarenesses.

Although defined in many ways, the aura is the energy field that surrounds all matter. Anything that has an atomic structure will have an aura, an energy field that surrounds it. Every atom of every substance is comprised of electrons and protons that are in constant movement. These electrons and protons are electrical and magnetic energy vibrations. The atoms of animate life are more active and vibrant than those of inanimate matter. Thus the energy fields of trees, plants, animals and people are more easily detected and experienced.

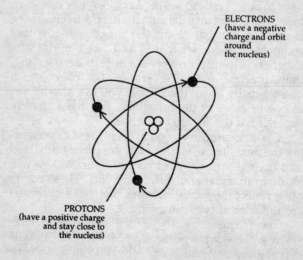

ELECTRONS
(have a negative
charge and orbit
around
the nucleus)

PROTONS
(have a positive charge
and stay close to
the nucleus)

The Energy Vibrations of Atoms

Have You Experienced the Auric Energy Field?

(If you can answer yes to any of these questions, you have experienced the interplay of an outside energy field upon your own aura.)

1. When you are around some people do you feel drained?

2. Do you associate certain colors with people? (For example, "You always seem like a yellow person to me.")

3. Have you ever felt when someone was staring at you?

4. Have you ever had an instant liking or disliking for someone?

5. Have you ever been able to sense how someone is feeling, in spite of how this person was acting?

6. Have you ever been able to sense another person's presence before you actually heard or saw this person?

7. Do certain sounds, colors and fragrances make you feel more comfortable or uncomfortable?

8. Do electrical storms (thunderstorms) make you nervous and edgy?

9. Do you find that some people excite or energize you more than others?

10. Have you ever walked into a room and tightened up, fidgeted or felt angry? Do some rooms make you want to stay? Leave?

11. Have you ever ignored or shoved aside a first impression of someone, only to find that it bears itself out eventually?

12. Are some rooms more comfortable and enjoyable to be in than others? Do you notice the difference in one room from the next? Did you ever notice how your brother's/sister's room feels different from yours? How about your parents' or children's?

The human aura is the energy field that surrounds the physical body. It surrounds you in all directions. It is three dimensional. In a healthy individual, it makes an elliptical or egg shape about the body (see the picture on page 5). In the average individual, it will extend eight to ten feet around the body. I have heard it proposed that the auras of the ancient masters could extend outward from the body for several miles. It is often believed that this is one of the reasons they could draw such large numbers of followers in any area where they traveled. It is worth noting that a common depiction of many masters included the halo, a portion of the aura that is most easily seen by the average individual.

Although the size and intensity of the auras of ancient masters cannot be verified, it is true that the healthier you are, physically and spiritually, the more vibrant your energy will be and the further the aura will extend out from your physical body. The more vitalized your auric field is, the more energy you will have to do the things you need and wish to do. The stronger your aura is, the less likely you are to be affected by outside force.

Auric fields that are weak are those in which outside influences are more likely to impinge upon you. This can result in being more easily manipulated and becoming tired more easily. Weakened auras can result in and reflect feelings of being a failure, health problems and an ineffectiveness in many or all life situations. As you will learn, control of your environment begins with control of your energy. Methods of strengthening and enlarging your auric field for various purposes will be explored in the last chapter.

The aura or human energy field is comprised of two aspects. This includes the energies of your subtle bodies, as described in traditional metaphysics (refer to the diagram on page 10). These subtle bodies are

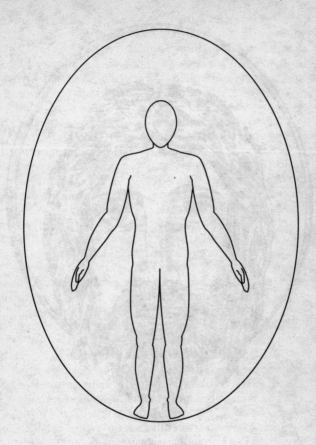

The Human Aura

The aura surrounds the physical body in all directions. It is three dimensional, and in a healthy person is elliptical in shape. The shape, the size, the colors and the clarity of colors all indicate specific things about your physical, emotional, mental and spiritual well being.

The Halo
The halo is common to most artistic depictions of ancient mystics and masters. The auric emanations around the head are the most easily detected by the individual. The healthier you are and the more spiritual you become, the stronger the light emanations from the body. The halo is often seen as a sign of spiritual illumination.

The aura is weakened by:

1. Poor diet
2. Lack of exercise
3. Lack of fresh air
4. Lack of rest
5. Stress
6. Alcohol
7. Drugs
8. Tobacco
9. Negative habits
10. Improper psychic activity

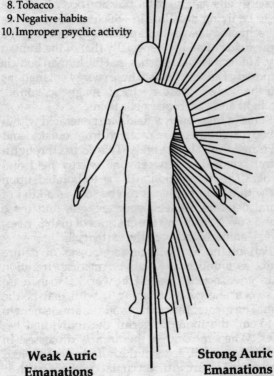

Weak Auric Emanations   **Strong Auric Emanations**

The stronger and more vibrant the aura is the healthier you are, and the less likely you are to be influenced and impinged upon by outside forces.

bands of energy of varying intensity that surround and interpenetrate with the physical. Their predominant function is to help coordinate and regulate the soul's activities in the physical life, but their aspects will not be examined to any degree in this work. For your purposes, it is enough to simply include them as part of the entire auric field.

The aspect of the auric field focused upon here is the energy emanations of the physical body itself. It is nice to be living in a time in which modern science and technology have the capability of verifying the energy fields of all life, especially that of the human body. Modern science teaches that the human body is composed of energy fields. These energy emanations from the body include electrical, magnetic, sound, heat, light and electromagnetic fields.

Some of these energy fields are generated within the body and others are received from outside and then transformed by the body. This occurs through a natural interaction between one energy field and another. This interaction will be elaborated upon later within this chapter. It can be seen as a kind of natural osmosis between your energies and those around you. You absorb the energies of plants, trees, flowers, animals and even the earth itself.

Part of the significance and power of nature totems, as found in the Native American tradition and in other societies around the world, is to increase one's own energy by aligning it with that of the totem. The greater the contact and the attunement to the totem, the more powerful the individual becomes. When measuring the aura is discussed in Chapter 4, you will see that the aura is stronger and larger when you are in direct contact with the earth or an element of nature. Measure the aura while outside in your bare feet and with shoes on. There will be a noticeable difference.

The energies of nature are easily absorbed and transformed by the body. A common form of healing and recuperation was to send an individual off to the ocean for convalescence. An ocean environment has the four basic elements of life. There is fire from the sun, air from the ocean breezes, the water of the ocean itself and, of course, the earth. The body of the individual is able to absorb and transform these into healing energies, strengthening the entire energy system—physically and otherwise. The association and contact with these four elements restores balance to the individual.

The aura, however, is not just comprised of energies absorbed and transformed from the elements of nature. There is also a subtle interaction of the body with the energy fields of the heavens. Stellar influences—as are often described in astrology—are also absorbed and transformed into energy expressions within the individual. Some planetary influences may affect an individual more strongly than others and be more discernible. Keep in mind that everyone has his or her own unique energy system, and the way it interacts and works with the more subtle surrounding influences will vary from individual to individual. With a little study and self-observation, though, you can increase your perception of these influences and learn to work with them more creatively and productively.

You need to know how your auric field interacts with outside forces and energies. You need to understand how your aura affects and is affected by the energies of others. You need to learn to recognize the limits and strengths of your own energy fields. You need to be aware of those times when it is important to strengthen, balance and cleanse them. You need to become sensitive to those times when your aura loses energy. For your overall well-being,

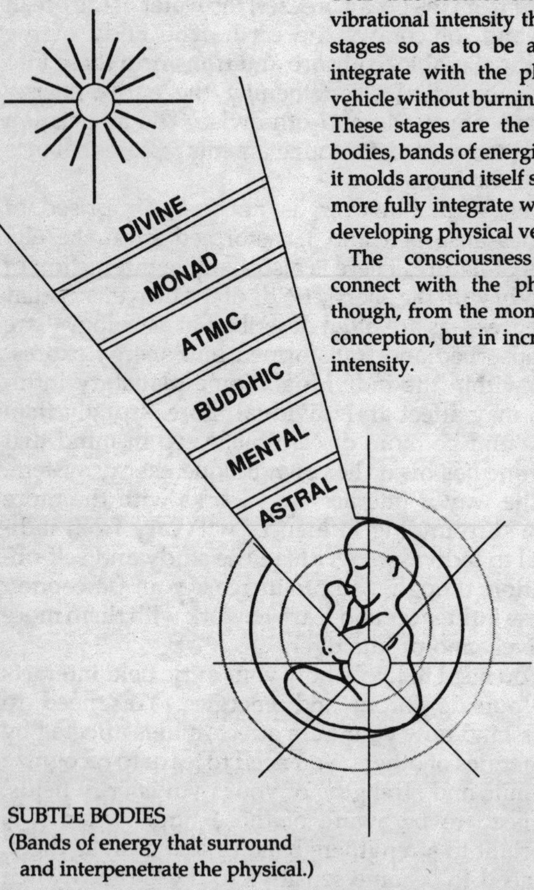

Your true spiritual
essence.

DIVINE

MONAD

ATMIC

BUDDHIC

MENTAL

ASTRAL

Your true essence slows its
vibrational intensity through
stages so as to be able to
integrate with the physical
vehicle without burning it up.
These stages are the subtle
bodies, bands of energies that
it molds around itself so as to
more fully integrate with the
developing physical vehicle.

The consciousness does
connect with the physical,
though, from the moment of
conception, but in increasing
intensity.

SUBTLE BODIES
(Bands of energy that surround
and interpenetrate the physical.)

The Subtle Bodies as Part of the Aura

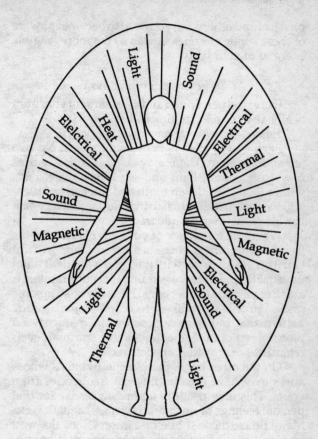

**Energy Emanations of
the Physical Body**
There are a variety of energy fields that surround and
emanate from the physical body. These include, but are
not limited to, light, electrical, heat and thermal, sound,
magnetic and electromagnetic fields. These are scientifi-
cally measurable, and they help to show that the human
body is an energy system.

physical and otherwise, you need to become as aware of these subtle energies as well as the more tangible energies of your body.

Characteristics of the Aura

Increased perception and awareness of your aura begins with understanding its basic properties.

1. Every aura has its own unique frequency.

Each energy field is unique unto itself. No two are entirely alike. There may be similarities. Auras may have sound, light and electromagnetic fields within them, but the strength and intensity of these will vary from individual to individual. Each person has his or her own unique frequency.

When the frequency of your aura is close to the frequency of others, there is a natural rapport. You "hit it off" more easily with those individuals. It is not unusual to find others assuming that such rapport is a sign of past-life connections. This may be so in some cases, but it is more likely to reflect a similar auric pattern that indicates a closeness in frequency on physical, emotional, mental and/or spiritual levels regardless of past-life connections.

On the other hand, there are individuals whose auras may have greatly different frequencies from yours. This may result in an instant dislike for that person, feelings of uncomfortableness, agitation etc. Many times, those subtle first impressions that you give and receive reflect the way your aura harmonizes in frequency with the other person. It does not always imply there is something wrong with the other person, but rather that the two energy fields are not in resonance with each other at this point. What may initially be a dissonance between two individuals can develop into harmony as the two are brought together over extended periods. This is often reflected in cases of individuals that epitomize the concept of "opposites attract."

You can learn to adjust and change the frequency of your aura with practice. Then you can fit and relate more easily and harmoniously with others. This is connected to ancient techniques of shapeshifting. You should be able to adjust the energy of your aura to the environment and the people. Often this occurs naturally, frequently as a mild form of self-protection. You can learn to consciously control it, so that you can interact with other fields as strongly or as gently as needed.

2. *Your aura will interact with the auric fields of others.*

Because of the strong electromagnetic properties of the aura, you constantly give off and absorb energy. Every time you come in contact with another person, an exchange of energy can occur. You may give them some (the electrical aspect), and you may absorb some of theirs (the magnetic aspect). The more people you interact with, the greater the energy exchange.

Unless you are aware of this exchange, you can accumulate a lot of energy debris by the end of the day. If you are unaware, by the end of the day you can be drained, and you may even have some strange ideas, thoughts and feelings running through your head. We have all had days in which we thought we were going a little bit crazy. These feelings may have nothing to do with you at all, but rather it may only have to do with the energy you have accumulated by contact with others throughout the day.

We have all known people who were draining to be around. Talking with them, on the phone or in person, can leave you exhausted. When the individual leaves or hangs up the phone, you often feel as if you have been punched in the stomach. This kind of exchange is unhealthy. What you experience is a

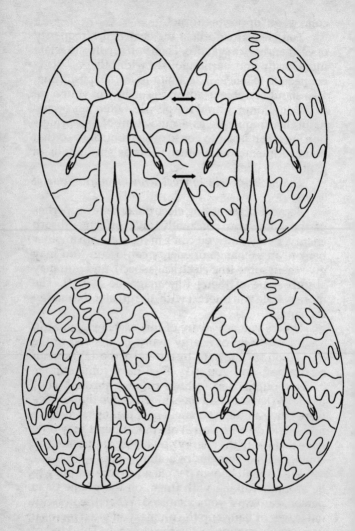

An Energy Exchange Through Interacting Auras

sucking off of energy from your aura. The exercises in the last chapter will help you to balance your aura each day, keeping it vibrant and preventing this kind of one-sided interaction.

3. *The human energy field can also interact with animal, plant, mineral and other energy fields.*

All matter, animate and inanimate, has energy fields because of its atomic structure. Animate fields are stronger and more easily detected, but both can be used to strengthen your own individual energy field.

Being around nature is balancing and cleansing to your aura. There is a lot of truth to the healthy habit of hugging a tree. Trees have dynamic energy fields, and they interact with human energy fields dynamically. Each tree has its own unique frequency, just as each human does. Because of this, different trees can be "hugged" for different effects. Sitting under a willow tree for about five to ten minutes will alleviate headaches. Pine trees interact with the human energy in a cleansing manner. They absorb and draw off negative emotions, especially feelings of guilt, from the human auric field. (The pine tree is not harmed by this, as it takes these negative energies and uses them like a fertilizer for itself.)

Crystals and stones have enjoyed renewed popularity in the '80s. This is because of their electromagnetic properties. The energy released by various crystals and stones are absorbed easily into the human auric field. There are exercises in Chapter 4 for measuring the aura. A good experiment to prove to yourself the effects of crystals and trees on the aura is through measuring. Hold a crystal for a few minutes or hug a tree for a moment and then measure your aura. Compare it to an original measurement. Your aura will have increased in size.

Animals also have auras that affect you. Research

is being conducted in several areas of the country in regards to the effects of pets on the elderly and the ill. Petting animals has been shown to lower blood pressure. It is balancing to the aura and stabilizing to physical, emotional, mental and spiritual energies. The aspect of animal totems was discussed briefly in the consideration of the first characteristic of the aura. It ties into this aspect as well.

4. *The longer and more intimate the contact, the greater the energy exchange.*

Your own aura will leave its imprint upon that with which you interact. This can be another person, a part of the environment or even an object. The longer and more intimate the contact, the stronger the imprint will be. The electromagnetic aspect of your aura is what causes you to magnetize objects and places. If you are used to sitting in a particular chair, you leave traces of your energy around it. It becomes *your* chair. If you grew up in your own room, you know that it has a feel that is different from that of your parents' room or that of your brother or sister.

Your aura charges the environment with an energy pattern in harmony with your own. Many individuals cannot sleep except in their own beds. Strange beds do not have energy patterns comfortable to them. The breaking-in period of beds, clothes, new homes etc. is the time it takes for your aura to magnetize and harmonize the environment or object with your own energy frequencies.

A child's blanket or favorite stuffed toy will become magnetized with the energy of the child's aura. The toy or blanket absorbs the energy. Holding the blanket or toy is a way for the child to recharge, balance and regain contact with its own basic energy pattern. This is why after a busy day of activity it is calming for the child to hold or snuggle with the toy or blanket. They draw on energy reserves that have accumulated in the toy or blanket. Children become upset when their blanket or toy is thrown into the washer because they recognize that the washing, cleanses the toy or blanket of the energy charge that has accumulated within it.

It is this same principle which lies behind meditation and prayer shawls and blankets. They are energized with a particular frequency of energy—that of meditation and praying. Thus each time one is used for that, that energy becomes even more magnetized and the individual finds it easier to achieve and hold a meditative state of mind.

The basis of psychometry (reading the vibrations from objects) is a direct result of the interaction of the individual's aura with that object. The longer the person has had contact with an object, the stronger it becomes charged with an energy pattern that is similar to that of the person. A sensitive person can then hold that object and become impressed with insights into the individual to whom it belongs.

The more you are exposed to certain energy patterns, the more you are influenced by them and the more they are influenced by you. If the energy field of another is stronger, it can easily bring your own into resonance or rapport with it and vice-versa. This is why peer pressure is a powerful influence. The energies of the entire group are stronger than that of the ordinary individual. The more contact between the group and the individual, the more the individual's aura will come into harmony with that of the group and reflect its unique characteristics.

Intimate contact, such as through sexual activity, can very intricately entwine the auric energies of the individuals. Sex creates a powerful and intimate exchange of auric energy between those involved. Such energy connections and "debris" can last much longer than those occurring through casual contact. They are not as easily or as quickly cleansed and balanced. No matter what you may have convinced yourself of, there is no such thing as "casual sex". Thus someone who is very promiscuous can entwine the energies of a variety of people on very subtle levels if the energy connections are not severed and cleansed prior to intimate contact with someone else.

The longer and more intimate the contact with another, the more subtle and powerful the interactions of the auric fields. Parents (especially the mother) share at least some of their auric energies with their children throughout their entire lives. In strong relationships, there is a dynamic entwining and sharing of these energies. Part of the mourning process at death involves the withdrawal of the deceased individual's energy from those he or she may have shared with. The closer and more intimate the relationship, the longer this untangling can take. Even in families where there seemed no great closeness, there will occur a vague sense of emptiness, as the energy of the deceased individual untangles itself and withdraws from those still in the physical.

5. *The aura—and changes within it—reflects physical, emotional, mental and spiritual aspects of the individual.*

The colors, the clarity of the colors, the size and shape of the aura etc. all provide information on the health and well-being of the individual. As you will come to understand later, seeing the aura is the easy part. Interpreting what you see is usually more difficult.

In general, a weak auric field makes you more susceptible to outside influence (see the diagram on page 20). This can be anything from being more susceptible to illness to emotional/mental imbalances. A good example is seen in large office environments. When you are rested, the noise within the office—the clatter of the typewriters and other office machinery—does not bother you. You can ignore it more easily. As the day wears on and your energy gets lower, the vibrancy of the aura diminishes. As it does so, you are more easily affected by the noises within the environment. They impinge upon you. They penetrate your auric field, creating irritation and imbalance. The more you are aware of this, the easier it is to take measures to keep your aura balanced and protected.

Every time you have a strong emotional reaction, there is a corresponding change in your aura. This may affect the color, shape or any of a variety of aspects. The same holds true for mental and spiritual responses. The activities in which you involve yourself reflect themselves in your aura. In Chapter 5, you will explore how to interpret your auric perceptions, particularly those associated with color.

The colors and their intensity can vary dramatically throughout the day. It all depends upon what is or has been going on in your life. There are usually one or two color vibrations that may remain more constant. These can reflect patterns that you may be involved in for a particular period of time. These colors can reflect periods of a month to a year. The quantity of the color can provide a barometer along those lines.

For example, an abundance of green in the aura extending four to six feet around the body can reflect a period of growth and change lasting for four to six months. Again, though, you cannot always lock yourself rigidly into this interpretation. In the course of a single day, there can be a variety of color changes, all superimposed upon the basic energy pattern that you are involved in at this point in your life. Within

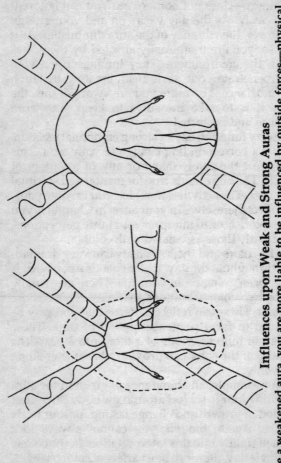

Influences upon Weak and Strong Auras

If you have a weakened aura, you are more liable to be influenced by outside forces—physical, emotional, mental and spiritual. A strong aura can repel or stop outside influence, preventing imbalances.

that green there can be various other colors and intensities, all reflecting different aspects of growth and change. It is this aspect that makes interpreting what is seen in the aura difficult. It requires some trial and error, along with development and use of the intuition.

EXERCISE
PUSHING AND PULLING ON THE AURA

This is an exercise that can be easily performed by you and a friend. It is a good way of proving that the energy field around you is entwined with the physical body and affects it powerfully

1. Have your friend stand facing away from you.

2. Standing about three feet away from your friend's back, raise your hands in front of you as if you are going to shove him/her (see the diagram on page 23).

3. Slowly extend your arms and hands as if pushing an invisible wall forward.

4. Once extended, pull back your arms and hands as if you were pulling back that invisible wall.

5. Repeat the movements. Push. Pull. Forward . Back. Make your movements slow and deliberate.

6. As you make these movements, you cause pushing and pulling upon the aura of your friend. This in turn results in his or her physical body swaying forward and back. With your pushing movement, the person's physical body will sway forward. With your pulling movement, the physical body sways backward.

7. The friend is placed with his/her back to you so that your pushing and pulling movements cannot be detected and thus influence or clue your friend unconsciously.

8. Sometimes the swaying that results is not easily detected by the individuals participating in the

exercise. If this occurs, include a third person as an observer. Have him or her stand or sit five to ten feet away, so that you and your friend are in profile to the observer. The swaying that results will be visibly detected.

9. Alternate. Have your friend push and pull on your aura. Place yourself in the observer's position. Remember that you are beginning a process to confirm the reality of the auric field surrounding the human body.

10. Sometimes it is good to place someone in front of the person whose aura is being pushed and pulled upon. This person serves as "catcher" to prevent falling from the swaying motion.

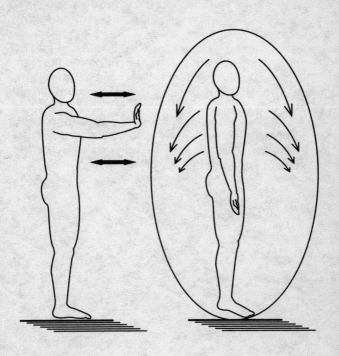

Pushing and Pulling on the Aura
Because the aura is a dynamic part of the entire energy
system, pushing and pulling upon it causes the physical
body to weave forward and backward as well.

2

Feeling the Aura

Most people can be placed into one of two categories when it comes to the aura. One group usually believes that there is no such thing as an auric field. The second category includes those who may believe there truly is an energy field but do not believe it can be seen. Fortunately, we are at a point where we can prove that there is an aura and that it can be seen.

Most people only see or experience as much as is necessary or essential to them and their immediate, individual lives. People today are very ignorant of the functions and activities of the physical body. There exists an attitude that we have physicians, so why take the time ourselves? Thus you give over your responsibilities and much of your innate power and control. When you are so casual about your own physical body and its energies, it is no wonder there is such strong prejudice about the more subtle energies of life.

This chapter is designed to increase your awareness and perception of the more subtle energy fields around you. It will help you to feel and to see the energy emanations of the body. It will help you to understand their influences upon you. Practice and persistence with these exercises is the key.

The exercises are organized in a progressive manner. They begin with simple energy exercises so that you can begin to feel and experience some of the more subtle auric energies. They build to exercises that will assist you in not only feeling the energies, but also actually seeing them as well.

Unfortunately, when it comes to the aura, we are often dealing with a person's belief system. Regardless of scientific verification, if the belief is held that no such thing exists, the task of opening new realization can be difficult. Most people grow up with little or no acknowledgment of the subtle energies of life. Any such experiences with them are attributed to an active imagination. These exercises will assist in breaking down those outworn, limiting thoughts and ideas. They will reawaken and expand the subtle perceptions that closed down in childhood. They will increase your sensitivity, and they will develop and strengthen visual awareness of the aura.

The time frame in which results will be experienced varies from individual to individual. Persistence is the key. Initially, some exercises will be more successful than others. Do not be discouraged at any failure during initial attempts to experience and see the aura. As with any ability, it takes time and practice. *Remember: Seeing the aura is natural to all of us!* The ability to do so has lain dormant for many years. You must begin stretching those unused muscles and abilities slowly and persistently. If you follow through and do not let yourself become discouraged, you will be successful!

Although the exercises can be enjoyable, keep in mind that there is a serious side as well. Learning to see the aura is a commitment to yourself and to others. Approach the exercises with sincerity and keep in mind that you are embarking on a life-long process of self-improvement. You are initiating a process that will enable you to know yourself and others more intimately. You are stepping out into areas that lead to sacred perceptions. Treat the process with respect.

The effects of the exercises are assisted when you learn the ability of relaxed concentration. Trying too hard can block your progress. Learn to meditate and relax the body before the exercises. Performing a short, progressive relaxation before an exercise is beneficial. Take a few moments, close your eyes and breathe deeply from the diaphragm. Focus on each part of your body, starting at your feet. Mentally send warm, relaxing feelings into that area of the body. See it, feel it, imagine it. Then move up the body, through each major muscle group, culminating at the crown of the head.

Take your time with this practice. Close your eyes and employ deep, rhythmic breathing. You may wish to use some soft music or environmental sounds to assist in the relaxation. The longer you take on focusing each part, the more relaxed you will become. The more relaxed you are, the better you will be able to concentrate. The more you are able to concentrate, the more sensitive you become to the subtle energies around you.

Relaxation creates a hyperesthetic condition. You become hypersensitive. If you have ever been jarred from a reverie or daydream by a phone ringing or a loud noise, you have experienced one aspect of this condition. When you are relaxed—in an altered state of consciousness—you experience outside energies more intensely. A phone ringing will seem louder. Smells are stronger. Light and colors become brighter. Because of this, relaxation will assist you in perceiving the subtle energies of the aura more easily. It amplifies your perceptive abilities.

EXERCISE #1
FEELING AND EXPERIENCING
YOUR SUBTLE ENERGIES

In this exercise, you are simply working to become more sensitive to the subtle emanations surrounding your physical body. This exercise can be performed by yourself, but it can also be adapted to practicing with a friend.

Your hands are points where there is a greater degree of energy activity. There are a number of these spots throughout the body. Seven of these are associated with the traditional chakra system (see page 29). The energy emanations are stronger around these areas of the body. Your hands, however, can become very sensitive to the subtle energies surrounding your body. They can be used to feel this energy as well as to project it outward. It is this ability that is known as the "King's Touch," the laying on of hands, the etheric or therapeutic touch in healing.

You will begin your exercises with the hands, as they are the easiest means of detecting the subtle energies of the aura. As you increase the sensitivity of one aspect of ourself, you will increase sensitivity in other areas as well.

1. Begin by making yourself comfortable in a seated position. Performing a relaxation exercise prior to this will assist you.

2. Rub the palms of your hands together briskly for about 15 to 30 seconds. This helps activate their overall sensitivity.

3. Extend your hands about a foot to a foot and a half in front of you, the palms facing each other. Hold the hands about two feet apart.

4. Slowly move the hands toward each other. Bring them as close to each other as you can without touching them.

5. Draw them slowly back to about six inches

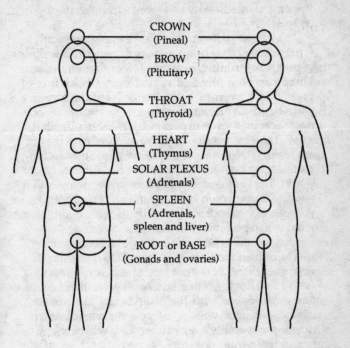

CROWN
(Pineal)

BROW
(Pituitary)

THROAT
(Thyroid)

HEART
(Thymus)

SOLAR PLEXUS
(Adrenals)

SPLEEN
(Adrenals,
spleen and liver)

ROOT or BASE
(Gonads and ovaries)

The Chakra System

The chakras mediate all energy within, coming into and going out of the body. They help distribute energy for your physical, emotional, mental and spiritual functions. The seven major chakras are points of greater electromagnetic activity within the auric field. The hands and feet are other points of great activity. The subtle auric energies are more easily detectable around them.

apart. Repeat this slow in and out movement. Keep your movements slow and steady (refer to the top of page 31).

6. As you perform this exercise, pay attention to what you feel or sense. You may experience a feeling of pressure building. You may have other sensations. These can be a sense of rubberiness, of tickling, of pressure or even of a thickness building between your hands. You may experience warmth or coolness. You may even experience a pulsating feeling.

7. Take a few minutes to try and define what you are feeling. Do not worry whether you are imagining it or not. Do not worry that it may feel different from what others experience; that is okay. Remember that you have your own unique aura frequency, and so you can experience it differently as well. Only what what *you* experience matters.

8. This exercise assists in developing concentration. It also assists in helping you to recognize that your energy field does not stop at skin level. You may wish to write down in a notebook your impressions and experiences with this exercise so that you can compare it later with what you experience as you develop this ability even further. This will help you to recognize your progress in experiencing subtle energies around the body.

9. Once you have completed the above exercise, you will want to take it a step further. Bare your weaker arm. Hold your dominant hand about a foot and a half above your bared forearm (refer to bottom of page 31).

10. Slowly lower your hand toward the forearm. Pay attention to anything that you might feel. How close do you come to the forearm before you can feel the energy from it? Remember that the feeling may be one of pressure, heat, coolness, thickness etc. It will feel much like what you experienced between your

FEELING AND EXPERIENCING
SUBTLE ENERGIES

The in and out movement of the hands causes the energy surrounding them to accumulate between them, making it more perceptible to you. The hands are becoming more sensitive to the subtle energies.

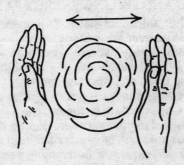

As the hands become more sensitive, you can use them to detect the auric energies emanating from other parts of the body as well. These detections may feel like heat, pressure, tingling etc.

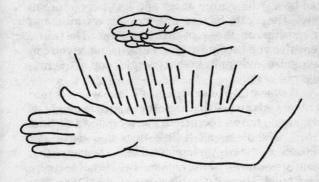

hands. It may not be as strong, but you should be able to feel it. If you cannot, slowly repeat it. Remember that you are reawakening your ability to consciously be aware of the subtle energies around you.

EXERCISE #2
SENDING AND FEELING ENERGY PATTERNS

An old occult axiom states: "All energy follows thought." Wherever your thoughts are focused, so are your auric energy patterns. Your aura adjusts its frequency in accordance with your thoughts. If you are focusing upon an important meeting, your aura will adjust its frequency to one of a serious vibration, a frequency appropriate to the occasion. If you are looking forward to your vacation, then by the time it arrives, your aura will have adjusted itself to a more relaxed, casual frequency. Learning to perceive and control your aura helps you to become more aware of energy patterns of thought that you project and have projected at you throughout the day.

You are exposed to the influence of extraneous energies constantly. These can impinge upon your auric field and affect your balance. These energies can be anything from anger and lust to pressure to buy. They can be the energies of warmth and friendship or those of manipulation. The more sensitive you become to your aura, the more you can recognize and control what energies you allow into and out of it.

We have all had experiences where we walk into a room and can feel that something, such as a fight or argument, has just occurred. The room has a distinct "feel". The air seems a little thick and tense. We become a little edgy ourselves. There are many such energy residues and projections that are not as easily detectable. These can influence and affect you very easily if you do not increase your awareness and

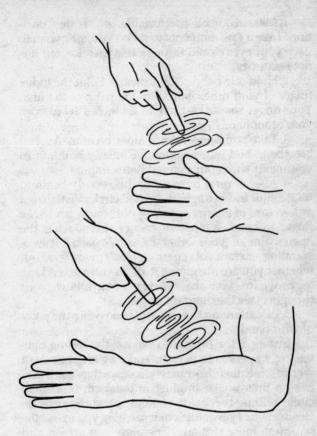

Sending and Feeling Subtle Energy Patterns

sensitivity to them.

In the following exercise you are working to increase your awareness of how outside energies can impact upon you. As you increase your auric sensitivity, you can block those energies that create stress and direct those that heal.

1. Make yourself comfortable in a seated position. Take a few moments to relax. You may wish to keep your eyes closed through this exercise, but it is not necessary.

2. Hold one hand palm upward. Point the index finger of your other hand into the palm of the first. Your finger should be three to six inches away from your other hand.

3. Take some nice, deep, slow breaths. As you breathe in and out, imagine the energy building in your hand with your pointed index finger.

4. After several minutes of this, slowly begin to rotate your index finger in a small circle. Visualize it as a stream of energy spiraling out from your index finger to create a circle of energy that touches the open palm of your other hand. Visualize it as a spiraling stream of energy. Don't worry about whether you are imagining it all, as you are working to prove to you that energy does follow your thoughts (see the diagram on page 33).

5. Pay attention to what you feel within the palm of your hand.

Just as in the previous exercise, the feeling may vary from person to person. You may feel a circle of warmth forming. You may also experience a thickness, a pressure or tingling in the form of a small circle within the palm of your hand. Sometimes closing your eyes at this point can help you to feel the sensation more strongly. The more you project and focus the energy with your mind and out through your index finger, the stronger the sensation will become.

6. Having worked with the palm of your hand, next perform this same activity upon your naked forearm. Visualize and send the energy out in small spirals to impact upon your forearm. Pay attention to what you feel. You will find with time and practice

that the kind of sensation you experience will remain much the same. What will vary is the intensity. Through exercises such as this, you begin to train yourself to recognize those feelings which let you know something is impacting subtly upon your energy field.

7. Another variation can be performed and practiced with another individual. Have the other person stand with his/her back to you. Hold your hand about six to twelve inches from your partner's back. Slowly direct energy from your hand to the other person's back, just as you did with your own arm. Use simple geometric shapes such as circles, squares, triangles etc. Have the other person try to feel what you are drawing upon him or her without touching that person. Keep repeating the movement with your hand. Concentrate as you project the energy.

8. Have the other person try to feel and identify the shape that is being drawn upon him or her. Pay attention to what is felt and experienced and compare it to the sensations experienced in the previous exercises.

9. Gradually increase the distance. How far away can you get from your arm and still feel the circles upon it? How far can someone stand behind you and project energy patterns upon your back and you still be able to identify them? Does it feel differently when the distances are extended? Pay attention to your responses. This increases your overall sensitivity to subtle energies and their effects upon your aura.

10. Slowly lower your hand toward your forearm. Pay attention to anything that you might feel. How close do you come to your forearm before you can feel the energy from it? Remember that the feeling may be one of pressure, heat, coolness, thickness etc. It will feel much like what you experienced between your hands. It may not be as

strong, but you should be able to feel it. If you cannot, slowly repeat it. Remember that you are reawakening your ability to consciously be aware of the subtle energies around you.

EXERCISE #3
DETECTING AURIC INTRUSIONS

For this exercise, you work to increase your sensitivity as to when outside energies touch, interact or intrude upon your own auric field. You will need a partner for this exercise.

1. Take a few moments to relax and then stand with your back to a wall with your eyes closed.

2. Your partner should stand on the other side of the room.

3. The idea is for the partner to silently and slowly step forward until you can feel him or her within your auric space. The partner moves one step at a time, pausing after each step.

4. Keep your eyes closed and feel the room with your mind and your aura alone. You may wish to place cotton in your ears and use blindfolds so that there are no audible or visual clues. Pay attention to how the room feels before you start. Note any changes you feel or experience.

5. How close does your partner get to you before you can feel it? What sensations are you experiencing? Can you feel when the partner moves to one side or the other? Add a third or fourth person. Can you feel their energies more easily if they move closer together?

6. This is a good exercise to experiment and have fun with as well. Don't be afraid to adapt it and change it. Mark a spot six to eight feet out from you before you start. As you close your eyes and so on, stay focused upon that spot. Can you feel when the partner crosses that invisible line? What does it feel

like? What happens if two people cross that line?

You are learning that you extend beyond the physical body. You are developing greater sensitivity to your entire auric field. As you increase this feeling of sensitivity, you will increase visual perception as well.

3

Learning to See the Aura

Seeing the aura is more a physical condition than a metaphysical one. Anyone can learn to see the aura. Interpreting what is seen is the difficult task, and it involves more of the intuitive and metaphysical aspects. These interpretations of what is seen will be covered in Chapter 5.

There are two ways of seeing the aura: intuitively and objectively. One way is neither better nor worse than the other, as long as what is seen is interpreted correctly. Both can be effective tools for insight, although physically perceiving the aura helps keep the "doubting Thomas" aspect of your consciousness out of your way.

In the intuitive method, the aura is viewed within your mind's eye rather than through your physical eyes. It involves learning to relax and visualize the individual within your mind. You must then ask your intuitive self about the energy of the individual's aura. What is the primary color of this person? What other colors are there and where are they most strongly located? What do these colors reflect about the energy of this individual on physical, emotional, mental and spiritual levels?

More often than not, these intuitive perceptions of the aura are as close and as accurate as the physical perceptions, if they are interpreted correctly. Thus one way of perception is not any better or effective than any other. However, the physical perception provides you with a more "tangible" awareness of the subtle energy fields.

These intuitive perceptions of the aura are easier to pick up from someone else than from yourself. It is very easy to delude yourself and picture what you want to see within your aura rather than what is actually there. It is always good to have some kind of confirmation or backup for your intuition. The use of the dowsing rods or the pendulum, as described in the next chapter, provides an easy means of objectively verifying your intuitive perceptions.

Anyone can learn to objectively see the aura as well. It is an ability that is natural to everybody. Most children see auras, but they are not taught to recognize them for what they are. It is not unusual for parents to comment about the colorful imagination of a child when the child refers to subtle impressions and awarenesses, be it in regards to the auric field or spirit guides. The child is often programed by parents and society to believe that such perceptions are imaginary and unreal. As this occurs, the child closes down and the innate ability to perceive atrophies. It can be re-awakened and redeveloped, however, no matter how long it has lain dormant.

You can train your eyes to take in and translate more of the light spectrum. To understand how this works, you must understand how your eyes work, particularly those portions of the eye known as the pupil, iris and retina.

As you can see by the diagram on the following page, the pupil is a small opening that allows light to enter. It looks black for the same reason that a distant house window looks black. The interior is not as brightly lit as the outside. The pupil of your eye can be adjusted to let in more or less light.

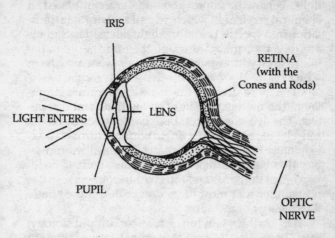

IRIS

RETINA
(with the
Cones and Rods)

LIGHT ENTERS

LENS

PUPIL

OPTIC
NERVE

The iris, a muscle of the eye, adjusts to let more or less light in through the pupil. This light passes through the lens and stimulates the retina. Inside the retina are sensitive nerve fibers called cones and rods. When the cones and rods are stimulated, chemicals are released which help you to detect and register light of various colors and intensity. The exercises in this chapter help stimulate brighter color vision and increased perception.

The pupil becomes smaller in bright light and larger in dim light. The iris opens and closes the pupil. The iris is a muscle which controls the amount of light entering the pupil.

As light is allowed in by the movement of the iris, it passes through the lens and acts upon the retina. The retina is the truly light-sensitive portion of the eye. It contains nerve cells called cones and rods which serve to detect specific colors and intensities of light. When the cones and rods are stimulated, a chemical is released which helps translate that stimulation into specific colors and light intensities. Signals are then transmitted through the optic nerve to the brain, and you are able to register what you have seen.

The more strongly the cones and rods are stimulated, the more subtle light emanations you can detect. The eye exercises in this chapter strengthen the muscles of the eyes. They help you to control your vision more than you might have imagined was possible. It is believed that you only use about 15 to 20 percent of the cones and rods within your eyes, so it is no wonder that most of us do not detect the subtle light energy of the aura.

Dr. Arthur Guyton, professor of physiology, says, "Between the limit of maximal dark adaptation and maximal light adaptation, the retina of the eye can change its sensitivity to light by as much as 500,000 to 1,000,000 times, the sensitivity automatically adjusting to changes in illumination." (*Basic Human Physiology*. W. B. Saunders Company, Philadelphia, 1971, page 427.) This simply means that you have the ability to perceive much more of the light spectrum than you have ever imagined.

EYE-CHART EXERCISES

A number of individuals have developed and used eye charts to exercise and strengthen the muscles of the eyes. As you strengthen the muscles, particularly the iris, you learn to adjust the amount of light you allow through your pupil to the retina. This ability can be developed to the point where you can discern subtle light emanations that you do not normally perceive.

The eye-chart exercises are physical exercises for the muscles of the eyes. They will strengthen your eyes to where brighter color vision occurs along with more subtle light detection. As with all physical exercises, you should begin slowly and easily. You do not want to strain yourself or the muscles you are developing. The exercises are most effective if done every day, possibly twice per day, for no more than a 10- to 15-minute interval. That is all the time necessary to experience results.

Each of the four charts can be made from simple poster board. They can be cut out and constructed in dimensions of about 18 by 18 inches. You do not have to hold strictly to these dimensions. They are guidelines. The charts should be large enough so that you can see them clearly when they are hung on the wall in front of you, six to eight feet away.

When hanging them on the wall, hang them at eye level. If you will be seated during the exercises, hang them at eye level with respect to your seated position. Make sure the area on the wall around them is clear so there are no distractions. A blank wall is best. Do not hang them more than eight feet away when using them.

1. The Spiral Chart

This is a chart which helps to strengthen the muscles of the iris. It helps to strengthen depth vision and helps keep both eyes working together. You see most things through both eyes. When you look at an object, both eyes are focused upon it. When you change your gaze from something near to something far or vice versa, the muscles in your eye change the shape of the lens so that the new object of attention will come into focus on the retina. As you get older, it is more difficult for your eyes to make this shift from far to near. It doesn't have to be this way.

For this exercise, focus on the center of the spiral. Concentrate upon it. See it as a point deep within the tunnel, created by the spiral itself.

The Spiral Chart

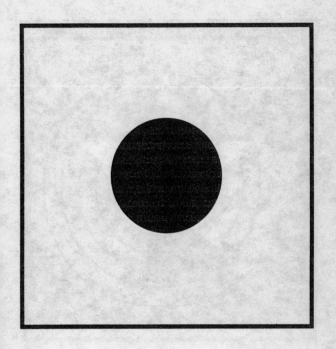

The Color Clarity Chart

Contrasting Light Shift

Now you want to draw your focus out of that spiraling tunnel, as if pulling that innermost point outward. Then shift, allowing your eyes to be drawn within it. In and out. Slowly. Mentally see it as if you are pulling the spiral toward you and then sending it away from you. It will begin to take on three-dimensional form.

If you have difficulty with this, focus your eyes on the outer edge of the spiral and follow it around and around until you are in the center. Then reverse the direction and allow yourself to come out of the spiral. Usually by the second or third time, you will begin to experience the in-and-out drawing effect.

Perform this exercise for no more than three or four minutes. You will feel the inner-eye muscles working throughout this exercise. If your eyes begin to hurt or strain, stop immediately.

2. The Color Clarity Chart

This chart is comprised of small (six-inch-diameter) colored circles against a white background. It is beneficial to make up as many different colored circles as you can find. Colored construction paper is effective and inexpensive. Cloth swatches can be used as well. You will need at least three colors, those of the primary set: red, yellow and blue. This exercise is even more effective if you construct inner circles for each of the seven colors of the rainbow (red, orange, yellow, green, blue, indigo and violet). Make up as many colors and shades as you wish.

With this chart you are teaching the cones to recognize subtle colors that do not usually register. Take time to set the chart before you and place each colored circle in the center, one at a time. Gaze softly at it for five to ten seconds. If your color has a specific name, mentally say it as you look upon it. You are teaching yourself to recognize and identify subtle color variations. This can be done periodically. While you are sitting and watching television, have this chart and the colored circles with you. Review several of them during commercials.

When you use this chart as a physical exercise, also use a second, all-white chart beside it. This second, plain white square should be hung level with the first, about one foot from it.

Focus on the colored circle and try to see it as if it were a three-dimensional colored ball or a colored hole within the white square. Use the drawing motion from the previous exercise and allow your eyes to be drawn within that red circle and then back out. Repeat this a number of times until you feel yourself going in and out of that circular hole.

Now bring your eyes to the outer edge of the colored circle and slowly begin to encircle it with your eyes in a clockwise direction. Repeat this four to five times and then reverse the direction for an equal number of repetitions. Make sure you are moving your eyes and not your head.

When the rotations have been completed, quickly move your focus to the blank white square. You will usually see an afterimage appear upon it (refer to the bottom of page 50). Afterimages are not part of the aura. They usually seem to float in front of the charts or the point of focus. The afterimage does indicate that you have stimulated the cones and rods strongly. Pause, noting any responses or effects. If nothing seems to occur, repeat the exercise again before moving on to another color.

Part of the phenomena of afterimages is the experience of complimentary colors. Oftentimes the color circle will reveal itself on the plain white surface in its opposite color. This can be likened to the astral counterpart of the color. As vibration translates itself and enacts itself upon the more subtle planes of life, its frequency is changed to that which is more reflective of the energy of that plane. What would be red on the physical may translate as green on the astral. They are opposite colors in the light spectrum, but they are actually just different frequencies. They are different expressions of the same energy applied to different dimensions of life.

This has been called the Law of Reversal, or a mirroring effect. If you look into a mirror, you see your image, but it is reflected in an opposite position. You are backwards. As you look and experience the subtle dimensions such as the astral plane of existence, this same effect occurs.

Remember that all planes and all energies interpenetrate with the physical, playing upon you and within you. Part of working to see and read auric fields involves increasing your awareness of these more subtle dimensions.

Eventually you will also see other colors surrounding this afterimage. These other colors indicate you are beginning to achieve results. They are subtle light emanations you did not detect during the initial exercise. Shortly after this, colors will begin to be observed during the actual eye rotation.

Close your eyes and allow them to rest. Then move on and repeat the exercise with the next color. Pay attention to what you experience. Do not be discouraged by failure to see colors or even afterimages during initial attempts. Practice and concentration will bring results. Go through as many colors as you can in a 10- to 15-minute period.

Colors and Their Astral Counterparts

Red — Green	Yellow Green — Red Violet
Blue — Orange	Red Orange — Blue Green
Yellow — Violet	Yellow Orange — Blue Violet

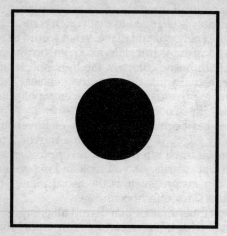

The Color Clarity Chart

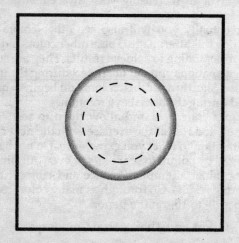

Afterimage on the Blank Chart

The afterimage of the color chart, although no part of aura, indicates stimulation of the cones and rods. However, this afterimage may reflect subtle colors not originally detected.

The contrasting focus exercise will stimulate a secondary shadowing of the star. This is the aura of the star becoming more visible.

3. Contrasting Light Shift Chart

This exercise chart serves two functions. First, it helps stimulate and exercise the rods of the eyes. The rods are what help you to detect various intensities of light. While colors register predominantly through the cones, light in general registers through the rods of the eyes. The more strongly the rods are stimulated, the greater the light spectrum that is registered.

Second, this chart will assist in developing the ability to "soft-focus" the eyes for seeing the auras around people. This soft focus is just a soft gaze at an area rather than at something specific within that area. We have all had times in which we hold that daydream look, as it were gazing off into nothingness. It is that kind of focus which you help develop and control through this chart. It is this kind of focus which will help you to see the aura around people more easily.

In this chart, a white star is placed within a black background. This contrast of white and black will cause the rods to learn to adjust more quickly. Ultimately, you want to be able to see the aura only when you wish. You want to develop the ability to turn on and off your auric sight at will. This chart assists you in this.

Bring your focus to the center of the star. As you focus upon the star itself, try and see it as an opening of light within the dark background. Use the drawing motion from the first exercise chart and allow your eyes to draw in and out of that star-shaped opening.

Now bring your concentration to the center of the star. Focus on the star and hold that focus for a slow count of 15. Now shift the eyes to take in the black background around the star. This shift is a simple relaxation of the eyes. You break the focus upon the star itself and allow the eyes to gaze softly upon the entire area around the star. You are shifting the eyes from a direct focus to a soft gaze that encompasses the entire area instead of a specific point.

Bring the focus back to the heart of the star itself. Hold for a count of 15, and then relax the concentration. As you work with this, pay attention to the eyes. You will feel the muscles shifting in and then pulling out.

If you have difficulty with this, bring the focus to one of the points and hold it at that point for a count of 15. Then relax, taking in the entire view of the chart. Move your focus back to that point and then relax it. If you wish, move your focus from point to point. Increase the length of time for focus as you do so.

As you work with this chart, you will begin to notice an interesting phenomena. As you move to the soft focus, you will begin to see a soft, secondary shadowing of the star forming around its edges. This is different from the afterimages seen with the previous chart. You may only see it at one or two angles of the star, but it will begin to appear. Initially, it will be almost gray in color, although, as you work with it, it will begin to reflect other colors. Blue is usually one of the first to appear. You are opening your auric vision (refer to page 42).

4. Eye Movement Chart

This chart is an overall exercise for the muscles of the eyes. It develops the ability for the eyes to register light and color more quickly. This is an exercise that should be done as quickly as possible. Speed is the key here. The more speed you develop in your eye movements, the more you will be able to detect things that are not as readily apparent. The quick eye movements stimulate greater cone and rod activity within the the retina. The faster you become, the easier it is to detect colors.

Begin at any of the five points on the chart. Then quickly move your eyes to a point that is opposite. Pause only a second and then sweep the eyes back. Move the eyes around from one point to the next. Make sure that you include vertical, horizontal, diagonal and circular movements.

This is a good exercise to do with each eye separately as well as both eyes together. Many people have one eye which is weaker than the other. This exercise can assist in overcoming "lazy" eye. It forces both to work to their maximum. Cover one eye with the palm of your hand. Then go through a variety of movements with the free eye. Then reverse it. Next work the chart with both eyes together.

As with all of the exercises, do not perform this one for more than ten minutes at a time. If you start to feel eyestrain, stop. Remember that you are stretch

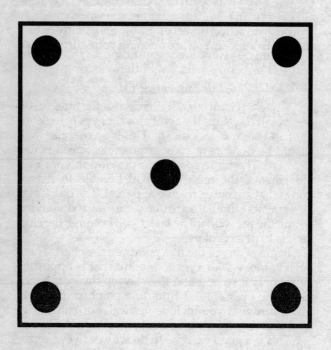

Eye Movement Chart

ing and strengthening eye muscles and activities which have lain dormant for a long time. Trying to do too much too soon is not beneficial. Be patient and persistent, and you will succeed. Remember it is natural to see the aura.

The Best Conditions for Seeing the Aura

Even with all of the scientific verification, there will still be people who doubt they can ever see the aura. For those individuals, I often recommend an exercise that helps prove its existence and your ability to see it. Lie back in an open area of grass on a warm, cloudless day. As you lie there, look at the distant trees. Let your eyes run from the base of the trees to the top. Gaze at the line the tree tops make against the blue sky. Don't force your gaze. Just relax. Try to take in as much of the sky at once as you can. Let yourself relax into a soft focus, like that daydream look of staring off into nothingness.

As you do this, you will become aware of a soft haze that follows the outline of the tree tops against the horizon of the blue sky beyond. Just passively observe this. It will be a soft, diaphanous color, lighter than the blue of the sky beyond. It outlines the trees against the sky. This phenomenon is most strongly visible in the spring when the sap and the life force of the trees are activated, and new growth and energy surges from the roots to the top branches. This is part of the aura of the trees!

What exactly are the best conditions for seeing the aura? This is an area of auric study that holds a lot of disagreement. Some say it is easier in the dark, because the subtle lights will stand out more. Unfortunately, the light energy given off by the body (photon radiation) is absorbed by the darkness. On the other hand, darkness forces the rods to work extra hard to give you "night vision". Others say that it is best in a brightly lit area, as the light spectrum has freer play and greater activity. In bright lights, the cones are excited and the higher intensities and the subtle colors are more easily detected.

I have found that there is a medium ground for seeing the aura more easily. Initially, it is most effective to use a dimly lighted room. You want to first start *seeing* the aura. As you develop the ability to detect it, then you can more easily fine tune it to determine the colors. So, for the beginner, I recommend starting with the dimly lit environment. A room at dusk is an excellent time and place to experiment. Dim light forces you to activate your night vision. It forces the rods to absorb and register more of the light spectrum, especially at levels not ordinarily apparent.

1. You will need dim light, a plain white wall and a piece of plain white cardboard. (It must be large enough to allow your hand to stand out against it.)

2. Take time to relax before performing this exercise. If you have been using the eye-chart exercises, you may want to do a quick abbreviated version of them as a warm-up.

3. Begin with your hands. Extend one of your hands out in front of you about a foot or 18 inches. With your other hand, hold the plain white cardboard behind it. This makes your hand stand out against the white surface.

With your hand flat against the white cardboard, the light emanations will be more easily detected as you softly focus your eyes upon it. It first appears as a soft haze. If you have been practicing, the haze will reflect colors as well.

With hands in front of you about three inches apart, begin your focusing. Concentrate first at the top edges of your hands and then soft-focus upon the entire area around them. Allow the soft gaze to look

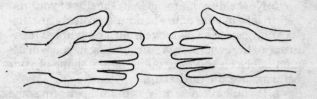

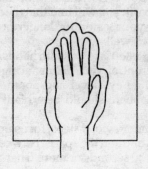

between and around. Concentrate. Then soft-focus. The aura of your hands will begin to stand out.

4. With your hand flat against the white cardboard, focus your attention upon the tips of your fingers. Hold this focus for about 30 seconds.

5. Now shift your focus from the tips of your fingers to take in your entire hand and poster board. Relax your gaze. As you move from a pinpointed focus to one of the general area surrounding it, you will begin to detect a soft haze outlining the shape of your hand against the cardboard.

6. If you have difficulty with this, perform some of the eye exercises with your hand against the card board. Focus in and out. Move your eyes around the edge of your hand. Shift from the concentrated focus to the soft focus. If you have been practicing, the haze will appear.

7. Pay attention to any colors you may detect as well, even if they are fleeting. You may see hints of colors or flashes, and there is often a tendency to discount them. *Don't!* As you develop this ability and learn to control it, you will find that the ability to hold the colors in your vision for longer periods of time will develop as well.

8. The next step is to use both hands. Extend them both out in front of you, palms facing toward you. They should be eye level and about three to four inches apart. There should be a blank wall behind them.

9. As in the previous steps, focus upon the edges of the fingers or upon the spaces between them. Hold this focus for 30 seconds or more. Then release it into a soft focus that encompasses both hands and the surrounding area. Notice the way the hands are outlined against the blank wall. Passively observe.

10. What you actually see may vary. There may be a soft haze that surrounds the hands. There may be

flashes of color or a steady color. It may take the appearance of a heat wave rising up off the street on a hot summer day. In the beginning, it is almost always a pale white or blue, almost colorless. As you develop your ability, the color, the clarity of the color and the vibrancy of the aura will become more discernible to your naked eye.

Seeing the Auras of Others

The next step is to begin working to see the auras of others. If you have have been working with the exercises, you should be able to start experiencing significant results within a month or two. It depends on your consistency of practice and your persistence.

1. Have your partner stand flat against a blank white wall. Using a dimly lit room is most effective in the beginning. Stand or sit eight to ten feet away. You must be able to see your partner from head to toe, as well as with a large blank area surrounding him or her.

2. Begin by focusing your line of sight at the forehead of your partner. From the forehead, circle the eyes around the body of your partner in a clockwise direction. Do this as quickly as possible, making several revolutions. At this point, you are simply exciting the cones and rods of the eyes.

3. Return your focus to the forehead or to the very top. Hold a concentrated focus on this point for 15 to 30 seconds.

4. Shift from a concentrated focus to a soft one that encompasses a wide area around the body. Hold this soft focus, passively observing. The aura of the head and shoulders usually stands out most strongly. Repeat as necessary. You are beginning to see the aura of others! (Refer to the diagram on the next page.)

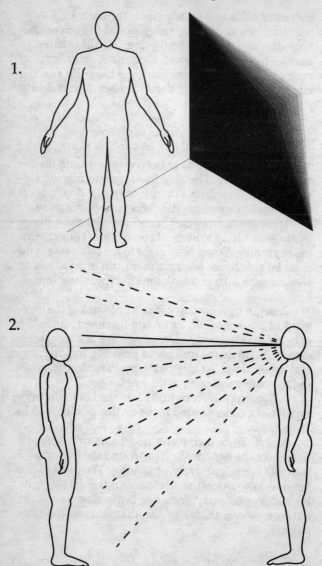

Seeing the Auras of Others

4

Measuring Your Auric Field

There are many new electronic devices which can measure the energy field around the human body. Unfortunately, the average individual will never be able to afford most of them. This does not mean that we cannot determine the size of our own auric fields. We can still measure the size and strength of them with a high degree of accuracy with devices that anyone can make and use. These devices are part of the science of radiesthesia.

Radiesthesia is a method of dowsing or divining to determine an energy radiation. It involves using a tool to measure the strength of a particular radiation. It is a system for translating unrecognized nervous-system responses to subtle energies into those which are tangible and visible. The two most common tools of radiesthesia are the dowsing rod and the pendulum.

Both of these devices assist you in communicating with levels of your mind that recognize the subtle energy fields you interact with. The fact that you are constantly interacting with outside energies has already been discussed. You are not always conscious of this fact, though, or you just don't acknowledge it. Dowsing rods and pendulums help you to link with those parts of you which are aware of this interaction.

Dowsing rods and pendulums are tools for communicating with your subconscious mind. The subconscious is aware of every interaction with outside energies, no matter how subtle. Through these tools, you open greater powers of perception. The dowsing rods and pendulums become an extension of your eyes. They are a link between the nervous system (and the subconscious mind working through it) and those energy fields you interact with.

The history of both methods is ancient. Although often thought of as strictly a psychic's tool, the dowsing rod and the pendulum are employed in many traditionally conservative arenas of life. They have been used in wartime to locate underground mines, tunnels etc. A number of utility companies train their repairmen in their use so that only the appropriate lines are dug up when repairs are necessary. Although some would scoff at their use, their accuracy is continually being verified by traditional scientific equipment and methods.

Your higher consciousness or intelligence communicates to you through your nervous system, sending you signals. Radiesthesia devices (such as the dowsing rod and the pendulum) amplify those signals of communication. You can therefore detect them and translate them. You thus open further channels of sensitivity to those subtle energies of life.

Making Your Own Dowsing Rods

When most people think of dowsing, they picture a man walking in a field holding the upper bars of a Y-shaped tree branch, trying to locate water or minerals. Dowsing has much greater application, though. A good dowser can not only locate subtle energy fields but also find the answers to questions.

The dowsing rods provide a link to your more

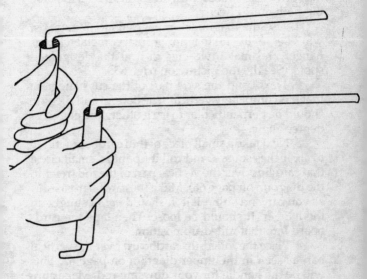

Ordinary Dowsing Rods

intuitive side. They are an extension of your eyes, providing visual clues that you can recognize more easily. The rods have no special quality of their own. They are simply tools to heighten your sensitivity.

The dowsing tools have been known by many names. The traditional wood or willow branch is the most commonly known, but anyone can make a set of dowsing rods that are just as effective. It is a simple task. About half of those who attempt it pick up the ability immediately. Others may have to practice for a while, but anyone can become skilled at dowsing.

The first step is to make a set of dowsing rods. This is simple. Everything you need to make a set can be found around the home. You will be shown how to make two sets, the second a little fancier than the first, but both quite effective.

1. Use the diagrams on pages 65 to 67 to assist you. Begin by taking an ordinary metal clothes hanger and make two cuts in it at the designated spots. (See the top picture on page 65.)

2. Next bend the side part of the cut hanger so that it is completely vertical. The bottom and the side should be perpendicular to each other, forming a 90-degree angle.

3. Next take a small piece of thin cardboard, three to six inches square, and roll it up into a small circle that can slide over the vertical part of the rod (refer to the diagram on page 66). Make the cardboard as stiff as you can and still roll it. It should *not* fit snugly on the hanger. It should be loose. Then tape the cardboard into that rolled-up position.

4. Place the rolled-up cardboard over the vertical bar, as seen in the upper diagram on page 67. This will be the handle for your dowsing rod. Make sure that at least one inch of the vertical bar is able to stick out of the handle. If it does not, trim the cardboard down to a more appropriate size.

5. Take that part of the vertical bar that extends out of the cardboard handle and bend it over so that the handle cannot slide off when the rods are used in an upright position. See the diagram at the bottom of page 67.

6. Repeat these steps a second time, making yourself a pair of dowsing rods. When finished, the rods should swing freely in the handles. They should

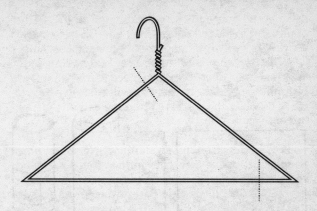

Step One: **Using an ordinary coat hanger, make two cuts in it at the points indicated in the above picture.**

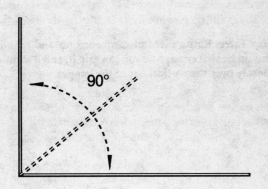

Step Two: **Bend the side portion of the hanger upright at a 90-degree angle.**

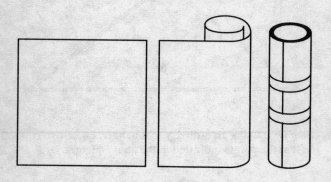

Step Three: **Roll a piece of cardboard up and tape it. It should be stiff enough so you can grip it, and it should fit loosely over the vertical bar of the hanger.**

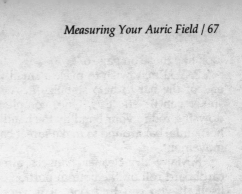

Steps Four and Five: Slide the cardboard handle over the vertical bar so that at least one inch sticks out. Bend this over to keep the cardboard in place. Turn the rod upright.

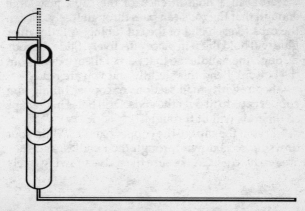

look like those on page 67.

7. You may wish to place a small weight at the end of the bar to help stabilize it. A small fishing sinker can be effective. Once completed, hold the dowsing rod in your hand by the handle. Swing the horizontal bar around to make sure it has freedom of movement.

8. Many dry-cleaner hangers already have a cardboard roll on the bottom portion of the hanger itself. If you can find one, it is very effective. It provides a firm grip and freedom of movement for the rod.

9. A more intricate version can be constructed inexpensively from materials found at any local hardware store. The handles particularly provide better grips and freer movement of the rods themselves. For this model, use copper materials. Copper is an excellent conductor of electricity and is thus even more sensitive to subtle energy fields and to the signals being sent from your own nervous system. Simply take three-quarter-inch copper tubing and have the hardware store cut you two sections about four or five inches long. You will also need two copper caps for each section of tubing. See the diagram on the following page.

10. Drill a hole in each of the caps, just large enough that the rods can pass through freely. Fasten the caps to each end of the cut tubing. A little super glue will hold them in place effectively. Slide the rods through the handles so that part of them extends out the bottom. Bend this slightly and you are ready.

Begin with small sections of copper tubing and copper caps to fit over the ends. Drill holes in the caps so the rods will fit through.

Fasten the caps to the copper handles. Slide your dowsing rods down through the handles, and they are ready to use. Make sure the rods can swing freely

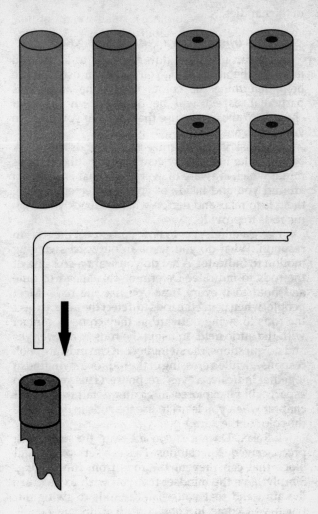

Dowsing Rods Made with Copper Tubing

in the handles.

Measuring the Aura With Dowsing Rods

You can use these dowsing rods to locate and measure the auric field. You can even use them to help determine the colors within the aura. This particular aspect will be discussed in the next chapter. You can also use them to give you clues to yes and no answers.

The task is to recognize that the rods are a link between the nervous system and the subconscious mind, which is aware of everything that is going on around you and inside of you. The secret to using them is to relax and decide what feedback you wish the rods to provide.

Have a mindset as to how you expect the rods to respond. What do you want an outward swinging motion to indicate? What do you want a crossing of the rods to indicate? Determine this ahead of time and hold to it every time you use the rods. Most people, when using the rods to detect the aura, expect the rods to swing outward as they come in contact with the auric field. In using the rods to answer yes and no questions, the swinging out can indicate "no" response, while a crossing of the rods or a swinging in together indicates a "yes" response. (This yes and no aspect will be explored in greater detail in the next chapter when you learn to use the rods to determine the color of the aura.)

1. Relax. Do not try to measure the aura with preconceived expectations. This can set up a mental block that can prevent the rods from functioning. Simply have the mindset that you wish to measure the aura and that you wish the rods to swing out when you come in contact with it. (Some people prefer that the rods cross when you encounter the outer edges of the person's aura. It is simply a matter

of personal preference. Just make sure that you have decided on the kind of feedback you expect from the rods before you start.) Relax and let the rods work for you.

2. Hold the rods lightly in your hands. They should be held out in front of you at shoulder height. The rods should be able to swing freely in a complete circle without touching any part of your body.

3. Have your partner stand about 30 feet away from you. The rods should be pointing straight out from you as you start.

4. Slowly and smoothly walk toward your partner. As you cross into the other person's aura, the rods will respond. This response lets you know the outer edge of his/her auric field. From that point you can draw a complete circle around the individual, as the size of that edge extends in all directions.

5. This means that the individual should be able to recognize when someone or something crosses that invisible auric line. He or she should be able to feel someone entering into his or her "space" at that point.

6. Practice with the rods. Measure the auras of your friends and your pets. Have your friend hold a crystal and then remeasure. Is there a difference? Is it significant? Try other stones. Have your friend stand barefoot while you remeasure the aura. What is the difference? Measure the auric field after hugging a tree. Measure it after eating chocolate. Measure your friend's aura while holding an apple. How does it compare to when he or she is holding a candy bar? Listen to a piece of heavy-metal music and remeasure. What happens to the aura? Then listen to a piece of classical music and remeasure. Try different fragrances. Experiment, have fun and learn.

As you begin to practice with the dowsing rods, you will begin to see certain patterns. You will re-

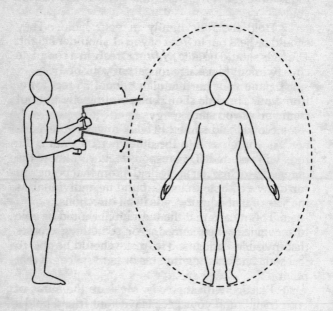

Measuring the Aura of Another
Stand about 30 feet away from the individual. Holding the rods out in front of you, steadily and slowly move toward the individual. As you cross the auric edge of the person, the rods will respond. You have found the outer edge of the aura. From that point you can draw a circle around the individual, letting him/her know the complete size.

ceive verification that certain things are beneficial to your energy fields and some things are not. You are beginning to open your perceptions of the subtle influences upon you. You are becoming reacquainted with your true self.

The Power of the Pendulum

Dowsing is usually considered the forerunner to the pendulum. The pendulum, though, works along the same principle. The pendulum simply interacts with a particular energy field. It operates on bioelectrical principles. The pendulum, like the dowsing rods, gives no answers itself.

The subconscious mind communicates to you through the nervous system. Because your aura extends in all directions around you, it is sensitive to all that occurs around you. The conscious mind is usually only aware of that upon which it is focused, that which is experienced through the five senses of taste, touch, sight, sound and smell. One of the greatest sensory organs you possess, however, is that of your skin. It is sensitive to many of the subtleties that are frequently missed by the other five senses. If you only look toward the five senses for your feedback, you can easily miss the subtle plays of energy within your life. The subconscious mind, on the other hand, is aware of all energy interactions with your own field, even those beyong the five physical senses. These interactions are assimilated and can be accessed and brought forth into conscious awareness through meditation, hypnosis and other techniques and tools for heightened consciousness. One such method is radiesthesia.

To understand this, you must understand more of how the subconscious mind functions, as opposed to the way the conscious mind works. The conscious mind is the seat of organized brain activity. It controls sense perception and expression. When you are consciously focused upon an activity, your brain emits electrical waves. The beta brain-wave pattern is a term commonly used to describe the wave pattern emitted in consciously directed activities. Because you have become overidentified with your intellectual faculties, you either ignore the subtle perceptions of life or miss them entirely.

An alpha brain-wave pattern occurs during relaxed states, and, in alpha patterns, the brain wave has a frequency of about ten cycles per second.[1] The more relaxed you become, the slower the brain-wave pattern and the more sensitive you become. Only about ten percent of your body and brain activity is a consciously controlled activity. Thus it follows that, if you are to reawaken the more subtle perceptions that register within you, you must learn to relax and access the subconscious mind.

The subconscious mind directs the autonomic nervous system. The autonomic nervous system regulates the functions of the vital organs and involuntary muscles. Normally, you are not aware of its activity, as it regulates activities necessary for life, reproduction and even self-preservation. These activities include, for example, the functions of the stomach, the lungs, the intestines, the heart, the liver, the eliminative organs, the reproductive organs and higher forms of sensation and perception.

This autonomic nervous syetem is a part of the central nervous system itself. In the body, the central nervous system acts as a coordinating system between the sense organs of the body and the muscles and glands. For example, if you prick your thumb with a needle, a message is carried from your organs of hearing to your brain and then out to a gland. You

---

1. Silverman, Robert, *Psychology*. Meredith Corporation, New York, 1971, p. 185.

say that you are emotionally upset.

The skin is a highly sensitive organ, and it has the capability of sensing subtle plays of energy surrounding us. An outside energy interacts with the autic field emanating from your skin and the entire human body, and the message is transmitted to the body and the brain. In such subtle perceptions as this, though, there is not always a recognizable response. The message, however, is held and can be accessed and brought into a more conscious awareness. It can be likened to having a message left on a recorder. If you know how, you can play the recorder back and learn the message. This is where dowsing and work with pendulums can be beneficial.

The nervous system of the body is still a great mystery, but we do know that it is a dynamic, delicate and sensitive communication system. It communicates with the subconscious mind and the higher inner perceptions. The dowsing tool or pendulum amplifies the signal from the nervous system to an involuntary muscle to create a tangible, recognizable response.

It is estimated that the subconscious mind controls 90 percent of body and brain function. It is also the source of your higher forms of perception and intuition (such as those that do not come through the usual five sensory organs), memory, creativity and abstract thinking.

The nervous system sends electrical signals and impulses, causing the pendulum to move. The swinging of the pendulum is an ideomotor response. It is caused by involuntary muscle action stimulated by the subconscious mind through the sympathetic nervous system of the body. The subtle messages received through the aura are lodged within the nervous system. Through dowsing techniques, the messages, in the form of electrical impulses, are released, stimulating the involutary muscle response that you can consciously perceive through the ensuing movement of the pendulum. The pendulum becomes a bridge between the subconscious and conscious minds.

Making your own pendulum is simple. You can use objects found around the home or you may purchase one at a variety of stores. Buttons, rings and crystals are commonly used as parts of the pendulum. The best pendulums are round, cylindrical or spherical. They work most effectively if they are symmetrical. The object used is attached to a thread, a string, a small chain, etc. The pendulum is hung freely from the end of the chain or thread, and its movements provide answers and input to subtle energy awareness. It is an amplifier. On the next page are four examples of common pendulum devices.

Learning to use a pendulum is easy. It requires only a little time and practice in a quiet place. It also requires the ability to relax. You must learn to keep the emotions out of the pendulum process, as they will short-circuit the electrical system.

1. The first step to using a pendulum is to get the feel of it. Take a seated position at a desk or table, making yourself comfortable. Have your feet flat on the floor. Rest your elbow on the surface of the desk.

2. Hold the pendulum by its chain using your thumb and index finger. Simply let the pendulum hang for a minute or two. Now begin to circle it gently in a clockwise direction. Allow it to come to a rest and then rotate it in a counterclockwise direction. Next move it horizontally, vertically and diagonally. At this point you are simply becoming comfortable with its feel.

Begin to form some experimentation with this. It takes only the most minute muscle movement to make the pendulum swing. You will find, as it is

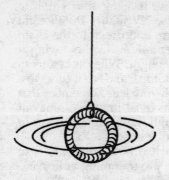

Simple ring on a string

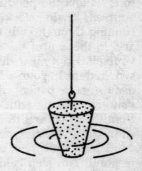

A cork, needle and thread

Quartz crystal pendulum

**Common necklace cross
and chain**

Common Types of Pendulums

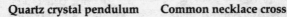

elaborated upon in point 8, that you can cause the pendulum to swing without making deliberate efforts. Allow the pendulum to hang still. Think to yourself, "Swing clockwise." Visualize the thought running through your arm and down to the chain and to the end of the pendulum. Do not swing it yourself. Do it all with thought. When it begins to swing, think to yourself, "Stop," and see it come to a dead stop. Be patient with yourself. Remember that you are working with electrical impulses sent out from the brain and through the nervous system to stimulate involuntary muscle action.

3. Now you must teach it how you want it to respond. This step is like programming your computer. You are telling it what kind of feedback it should give to you. You want to be able to understand its movement when you ask it a question. You want to let the subconscious know the kind of movements you expect to receive. On the following page is a sample chart you can use for this programming procedure. Use this one or draw on similar to it.

Begin with the two intersecting lines, as seen in the top diagram. Lay it flat on the desk and dangle the pendulum over the center. Tell yourself out loud, "When I ask a question and the answer is yes, you will make the pendulum move (direction) " (in this case, up and down along the vertical axis). At this point move your pendulum in the vertical line. Let it swing softly, repeating the above statement.

With this exercise, you are establishing the vocabulary for the communication process. Test this vocabulary. Ask yourself a question to which you know the answer is "yes," but do not consciously move the pendulum this time. Let the inner workings of the nervous system create the phsycal response. Use questions such as, "Is my name [place your name here]?" or "Am I ___ years old?" Doing this not only

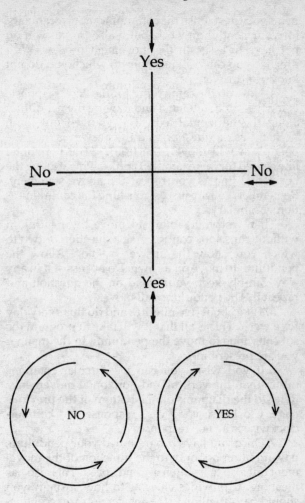

Programming the Pendulum Movements

helps you to establish the communication vocabulary for your pendulum work, but it also proves you do not have to assist in the movement process. With practice you can use questions to which you do not know the answer.

4. Now do the same thing for the "no" response, using the same statement and moving the pendulum along the horizontal axis. Tell yourself out loud, "When I ask a question and the answer is 'no,' the pendulum will move [direction]." (The horizontal line is used for this example.) Softly swing it along the horizontal line as you repeat the above statement. Remember, you are just establishing the communication vocabulary.

Then test your ability to move the pendulum without conscious control. Ask a question or two to which you know the answer is "no." Allow the pendulum to move on its own. Do not assist it in any way. Simply keep your mind on the question and repeat it. The pendulum will move.

5. Take about five minutes and do this every day for a week. This is all that it will take to program the subconscious to move the pendulum in the manner you are prescribing.

6. If you wish, you can use circular rotations rather than the vertical and horizontal movements. Refer to the diagrams on the bottom of the previous page. Clockwise is a "yes" response and counterclockwise is a "no" response.

7. Once you have programmed your pendulum, pay attention not only to the direction of the movement but also to its intensity and speed. This also has meaning. It provides clues as to how strongly you should pay attention to the answer you are receiving.

8. As you begin to program the pendulum, test it. Prove to yourself that it will move without your conscious physical assistance. Use the intersecting

lines. Rest your elbow comfortably on a flat surface. Let the pendulum hang still and then think to yourself the word "yes." Repeat it in your mind and let your eyes look up and down the "YES" line. Do this until the pendulum swings up and down on its own. It will only take a minute or two. Stay relaxed.

Now think to yourself "stop." As the pendulum comes to rest, repeat this procedure, using the word "no" and the "NO" line. Then do the same thing with the circles in both directions. You are learning to make it move with just the mind.

9. You must learn to ask yourself yes and no questions. The more specific, the better the response. For example, some people ask their pendulum if a certain food is edible. The pendulum may give a positive response. But if the question is phrased, "Is this food beneficial for me?" the pendulum may give a negative response. Experiment with it. Ask yourself questions which have definite "yes" and "no" answers:

- Have I lived before?
- Is my promotion going to come through this week?
- Have I had psychic experiences before?
- Is my dream telling me something I am ignoring?
- Is _____ going to call tonight?
- Do I have a soul?
- Should I start a new study?

10. It is important to keep the emotions out of the asking process. Some people will not relax, and thus the pendulum only responds the way they want it to. If you relax and stay as unemotional as possible, the responses will become very accurate. The more you keep the conscious mind out of the process, the

stronger and greater the perceptions will come. Remember that, with alpha brain-wave patterns — those that occur when you are relaxed — you become more sensitive to the subtle energy interactions with your auric field. When you are in a beta brain-wave pattern — consciously focusing — your perceptions are more often limited to those of the five senses alone.

Checking the Aura with a Pendulum

Measuring the size of an aura with a pendulum is not as easy as with the dowsing rods, but it can still be done. There are actually two ways of doing it, both of which can support each other.

The first is simply using a questioning approach. Use your "yes" and "no" charts. Ask yourself questions about the size of your aura. "Is my aura 15 to 20 feet?" "Is my aura 10 to 15 feet?" "Is the size of my aura between 0 and 10 feet?" Begin with general questions such as these, and then narrow it down with even more specific questions. "Is my aura 11 feet?" "Is my aura 8 feet?"

The second method is similar to that used with the dowsing rods. Have the individual stand about 20 feet away. Take a few moments to relax. Tell yourself and the pendulum that you want to have indications about the other person's aura. This way it will not pick up on your own.

Slowly and gently step forward. Because you are moving your body, there is a greater likelihood of you causing it to sway. For this reason, it is best to use a circular rotation to indicate contact with the other's aura. The positive response (clockwise movement) is effective.

After each step, pause, allowing the pendulum to rest and then respond. Although it is a little slower, you can still use it effectively. Although not 100

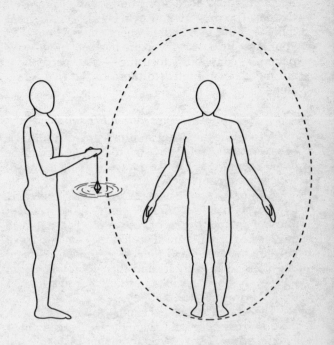

Measuring the Aura with a Pendulum

Although not as easy or as quick as the dowsing rods, this method can still be effective. With each step closer, pause and allow the pendulum to rest before it gives you the programed response. It is effective to use a clockwise movement as an indicator of contact with the edge of the aura.

percent accurate, you are increasing your awareness of your subtle energies.

5

The Meaning of Colors in the Aura

Color is a an intimate part of our lives. It affects us all and it reflects us all. It is used to describe our physical health, our moods, our attitudes and even our spiritual experiences. Listen to people speak and notice how often color is used as a part of their descriptive vocabulary.

"I'm in the pink today."

"He was so angry he turned red."

"She was feeling a little blue."

"They are just green with envy."

"Oh, he has a yellow streak down his back."

"It was a golden experience."

Color is a property of light. When light is broken down into different wavelengths we end up with different colors. It is like holding a prism up to the sunlight. It will display a rainbow on an opposite surface. Those seven colors of the rainbow are only a small fraction of the light spectrum. There are a multitude of shades and variances of each color.

The energy of an aura reflects itself in light and color. The color, its clarity and its location all indicate different things about a person's physical, emotional, mental and spiritual well-being. As you work with the exercises in this book, you will begin to visibly detect the colors of the aura. Until then, you can use the dowsing rods and pendulums to help you identify the colors of the aura. Determining the colors is the easy part. The difficult part is understanding and interpreting those colors.

We are all sensitive to color. We are also sensitive to what it may reflect. We just have not given it much conscious attention. We have all had experiences where we wondered about a friend because his or her "color" was a bit off. We have also heard comments about how the color of a blouse or shirt is wonderful for someone or washes the person out. Many times these comments reflect unconscious impressions of auras. They just have not registered as such.

Different colors reflect different attitudes, moods and energy patterns. Although you can identify generally what certain colors reflect, you must keep in mind that there are a multitude of shades within a particular color's spectrum. There are many shades of yellow, green etc. Understanding the significance of those shades takes time and practice.

In determining the colors within the aura, there are certain guidelines to keep in mind:

1. Those colors closest to the physical body usually reflect physical conditions and energies. The outer colors reflect emotional, mental and spiritual energies that can be affecting those physical colors.

2. The clearer and more pastel the colors, the better. Muddier and thicker colors can reflect imbalances, overactivity and other possible problems in the area to which the colors are connected.

3. Dark colors that are also bright can indicate high energy levels. This is not necessarily negative. You do not want to jump to conclusions.

4. There is often more than one color in the aura. Each color will reflect different aspects. You must learn how these different colors interact and what kind of effect that combination can have. Again, that takes time and practice.

5. When you start seeing other people's auras, keep in mind that you are looking at them through your

own aura. To interpret what you are seeing, you need to be aware of your own aura. Using the earlier eye exercises can assist you in seeing your own aura within a mirror. If your aura is predominantly yellow and the other person's is blue, you may actually see green. Yellow and blue combined make green. Often the subconscious mind is aware of this and makes that adjustment naturally, but you must be careful about jumping to conclusions.

6. It is important not to make judgments of people based on what you see in their auras. What you see and how you interpret it depends a great deal on your state of mind at the time. Consider the pros and cons of what is associated with that color, along with specific areas to which it is connected. You do not have the right to tell someone else what to do. Bring up the observations, explain possible significances and then let the other person make his or her own decisions and choices.

7. Learn to use your own intuition in interpreting. Ask the individual questions about what you are observing and what you think it might relate to. Only in this way, through the other person's feedback, can you develop criteria for your interpretations. Remember that the color, the location and the clarity can all indicate different things. Your task is to learn to synthesize them.

8. Auras change frequently. The colors closest to the body (extending out about a foot to two) can go through many changes in a single day. Every strong emotion and every strong physical or mental activity can result in color and light fluctuations in the aura. Our auras change as we go through life, as well. As you develop the ability to see the aura, you will find that an individual has a predominant color or colors that remain consistently within their auric field (although there may be shade variations). What are the secondary colors and what is their relationship to the primary tones?

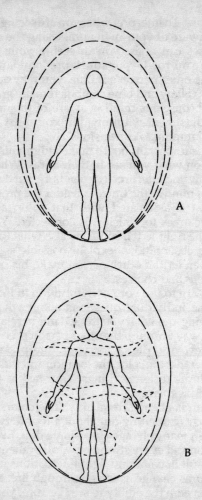

The Appearance of Colors in the Aura

Colors may take different forms, shades and positions around the body (figure B) or they may reflect themselves in softly blending bands of color (figure A).

9. Usually the first color or shades to appear are shades of gray and light blue. Do not be discouraged, however, if the colors do not become readily apparent. As you work with the exercises, this will change. Usually in the beginning people are very persistent, but they also expect results within a certain time frame. If the results do not occur quickly enough or strongly enough within that time, they become discouraged.

Set no time limits on yourself. Use the exercises every day. Only by exercising and stretching your perceptions every day do you open to effective results. Performing them two or three days in a row, then skipping a week and then going back to them will not bring results. You must be consistent. If you are, you will have some visual success within four to six weeks. At the very least, you will begin to see the aura, even if no colors become visible. Most people with whom I have worked begin to achieve excellent results within one to six months, but *it only takes a month to confirm that the process works!*

10. As you begin to develop your auric vision, you will begin to see auras around everyone and everything. This can be distracting. The exercises in this book are designed to help you develop the ability to turn your auric vision on and off at will. Remember that you do not have the right to be tuning into other's energies without their permission. In many cases it is like reading their mail. Even if you do perceive something, you do not have the right to reveal it unless you are invited to do so. Use your vision responsibly.

The Meaning of Colors

Color can be constructive or destructive. It can stimulate or depress, repel or attract. It can even be male or female in its character. It can reflect positive or negative, and when perceived within the aura it provides a key to the personality, moods, maturity and health of the individual. It reflects physical and spiritual aspects.

It takes a great deal of practice to interpret the color shades seen within the aura. Each color has its general characteristic, but each shade of that color changes that characteristic a little. The location of the color, the intensity and even the form the color takes in the auric field must be considered.

This text is not intended to provide all of the subtle nuances of color interpretation within the auric field. You will examine basic colors and the energies they commonly indicate on physical and other levels. This gives you a starting point to begin to understand what is revealed by the colors of the aura.

The colors closest to the body reflect aspects of the individual's physical condition. They also indicate those energies manifesting and pressing most currently within his or her life. The colors and energies further away often indicate the energy that the person will be moving into within his or her life. With practice, you will be able to determine time elements of certain energy patterns by the color and the location of the color with respect to the physical body.

The Rainbow Colors

Red

Red is the color of strong energy, fire and primal creative force. It is the life-promoting energy. It is hot. It can indicate strong passion, mind and will. It is a dynamic color that can reflect anger, love, hate and unexpected changes. It can indicate new birth and transmutation.

It is a color that affects the circulatory system of the body, the reproductive system (sexual energy) and an awakening of latent abilities and talents.

Too much red or a muddiness can reflect over-stimulation, inflammation or imbalance. It may reflect nervousness, temper, aggression, impulsiveness or excitement.

Orange

Orange is the color of warmth, creativity and emotions. It is an indication of courage, joy and socialness. It is a color which can reflect an opening of new awareness—especially to the subtle realms (the astral plane) of life.

Depending on the shade, it can also indicate emotional imbalances and agitation. Some of the muddier shades of orange can reflect pride and flamboyance. It may reflect worry and vanity.

Yellow

Yellow is one of the first and the easiest aura colors to be seen. Pale yellow around the hairline can indicate optimism. Yellow is the color of mental activity and new sunshine. It can reflect new learning opportunities, lightness, wisdom and intellect. The more pastel shades often reflect an enthusiasm for something in life, the power of ideas and spiritual development (especially in the pale yellow to white spectrum). Yellow is a color which represents the power of ideas and awakening psychic abilities and clairsentience.

Deeper and muddier shades of yellow can reflect excessive thinking and analyzing. It can reflect being overly critical, feelings of being deprived of recognition and being dogmatic.

Green

Green is the color of sensitivity and growing compassion. It reflects growth, sympathy and calm. It can reflect a person who is reliable, dependable and open-minded. Bright greens moving toward the blue spectrum in the aura indicate healing ability. It is a color of abundance, strength and friendliness.

The muddier or darker shades of green can reflect uncertainty and miserliness. The muddier shades often reflect jealousy and possessiveness as well. It can indicate self-doubt and mistrust.

Blue

Blue, next to yellow, is one of the easiest colors to see in the aura. It is the color of calm and quietness. It reflects devotion, truth and seriousness. It can indicate the ability for clairaudience and for the development of telepathy.

The lighter shades of blue reflect an active imagination and good intuition. The deeper shades of blue can indicate a sense of loneliness, which on one level reflects a life-long quest for the Divine. The deeper shades of blue reflect levels of devotion. Royal blue shades indicate honesty and good judgment. They can also indicate the person has found or is about to find his or her chosen work.

The muddier shades of blue can reflect blocked perceptions. They can indicate melancholy, rushing and worrying, domineering, fearfulness, forgetfulness and oversensitivity.

Violet and Purple

Violet is the color of warmth and transmutation. It is the color for the blending of the heart and the mind, the physical with the spiritual. It reflects independence and intuition, as well as dynamic and important dream activity. It can reflect one who is searching. The purple shades often reflect an ability to handle affairs with practicality and worldliness. The paler and lighter shades of violet and purple can reflect humility and spirituality. The red-purple shades can indicate great passion or strength of will. They may also reflect a need for greater individual effort.

The darker and muddier shades can reflect a need to overcome something. They can also reflect intense erotic imaginations as well. Tendencies toward being overbearing, needing sympathy and feeling misunderstood are also reflected in muddier shades.

Other Colors of the Aura

Pink

Pink is a color of compassion, love and purity. It can reflect joy and comfort and a strong sense of companionship. When seen in the aura, it can indicate the quiet, modest type of individual, along with a love of art and beauty.

Depending on the shade of pink, it can also reflect an immaturity, especially the muddier shades. It can reflect truthfulness or a lack of it. It can also reflect times of new love and new vision.

Gold

Gold is a color that reflects dynamic spiritual energy and a true coming into one's own power. It reflects the higher energies of devotion and a restoration of harmony. It indicates strong enthusiasm and great inspiration. It indicates a time of revitalizing.

Muddier shades of gold can indicate the person is still in the process of awakening higher inspiration and has not clarified it yet within his/her life. It reflects the alchemical process still being active; i.e., the person is still working to turn the lead of his/her life into gold.

White

White is often seen in the aura, prior to any actual colors. It is often seen as a diaphanous shade. White has all colors within it, and when it does appear strongly within the aura, it is often in conjunction with other colors. This is how you can know whether it is an actual energy color or just a poor perception of the aura. When the white does stand out as a color in the aura, it reflects truth and purity. It indicates that the energy of the individual is cleansing and purifying itself. It often reflects an awakening of greater creativity as well.

Gray

Gray is a color of initiation. It can indicate a movement toward unveiling innate abilities. Those shades of gray that lean more toward the silver reflect an awakening of the feminine energies. These are the energies and abilities of illumination, intuition and creative imagination.

The darker shades of gray can indicate physical imbalances, especially if seen next to specific areas of the physical body. They can also indicate a need to leave no task undone. Much gray in the aura can indicate a person who is secretive and who is the lone wolf type.

Brown

Brown often appears in the auric field. Although many people think of it as reflecting a lack of energy or an imbalance, this is not always so. Brown is the color of the earth. When it shows itself in the aura, especially in areas above the head and around the feet, it can reflect new growth. It indicates establishing new roots and a desire to accomplish. It is a color that can reflect industry and organization.

On the other hand, brown across the face or touching the head may indicate a lack of and need for discrimination. If seen in the areas of the chakras, it can indicate that those centers need to be cleaned. It will reflect in such cases a clogging of their energies. Brown is often difficult to interpret, as it can easily reflect problem areas in the physical, but you must be careful about jumping to conclusions when you see it. Feedback from the other person is the best means of understanding it.

Black

Black is one of the most confusing of colors in the auric spectrum. I have heard individuals say that, when black shows up in the aura, it is an indication of death or terrible disease. I have *not* found that to be true.

Black is a color of protection. It is a color which can shield an individual from outside energies. When seen in the aura, it can reflect that the person is protecting himself or herself. It can also indicate that person has secrets. There is nothing wrong with that, as long as it is not taken to extremes. Black can also indicate that a new understanding of burdens and sacrifices is going to manifest.

Black can also indicate imbalances. Physical imbalances often show up as black or darkened areas in the aura around the physical body. The location provides clues to this. In the outer edges of the aura, black can indicate holes in the auric field. I have seen this in the auras of those who were victims of child abuse* and those who are or were strong substance abusers (alcohol, drugs, tobacco etc.).

Silver Twinklies

Another aspect that I have observed should be mentioned. I have often seen within the aura what look to be soft, twinkling lights. They are usually very sparkly and silver in color. I have found that they indicate one of several things. These "twinklies," as I call them, are almost always a sign of great creativity and fertility. When they appear within the auric field of a person, it indicates that greater creativity is being activated within the individual's life.

I have seen these most frequently around women,

---

* In cases such as child abuse, the consciousness literally ejects itself from the body and out of the auric field during the abuse. The more frequently the abuse occurs, the more well-formed the hole becomes. Because of this hole and this ejection of consciousness, many individuals do not always remember much of the abuse. Also the aura will then continually leak energy, and the individual becomes susceptible to a wide range of physical, emotional and mental imbalances throughout his or her life. This tear in the aura is difficult to heal. Counseling and some of the exercises in the next chapter can assist in sealing the aura. Caution must be used in jumping to conclusions about abuse simply based upon what is seen in the aura. Only someone very well trained should even broach such a subject to someone else, and then only under very controlled, therapeutic circumstances.

but they are not confined solely to them. When I do see them around a woman whose aura I am reading, I will ask her if she is pregnant. These twinklies are always present around pregnant women and women who have delivered a child within the past six to nine months. You must remember, though, that not everyone that has the twinklies is pregnant, even though most pregnant women have them in the aura.

My own theory is that these twinkling lights indicate the activation of creativity and fertility within the individual's life. That creativity and fertility, however, can take a number of forms. They do not have to represent pregnancy. However, my own theory is that, when this creativity becomes so active that it shows up as lights in the auric field, it draws new souls close to that individual. Then, if the opportunity arises, they "slip in."

If the person I am reading is not pregnant when I have observed these twinklies, I will caution her to be extra careful over the next six to nine months, as there is a greater likelihood for pregnancy to occur. Forewarned is forearmed, so to speak.

If the fertility does not culminate with a physical pregnancy, then it will play itself out in another area of the individual's life. Usually within nine months, ten at the outside, something will be born into the person's life that ultimately will be as life-changing as a new child. A positive, beneficial door will open within the individual's life. It may take as long as six months for events to play themselves out fully, once that creative opportunity arrives, but it is usually very dynamic and very positive.

As you develop your auric sight, you will become aware of the subtle differences in color. A study of chromotherapy and color will assist you not only in becoming more sensitive to it, but also to understand its significance.

Determining Primary Colors of the Aura

Until you develop the ability to see the colors of the aura, you can still determine the primary ones through radiesthesia. You can use your dowsing rods or your pendulum. Remember that the subconscious is already aware of the energies of the aura. You just have not been able to consciously and visibly perceive them. The dowsing rods and pendulum help you to extract those subconscious perceptions and bring them out into your conscious awareness.

You can use the charts on the pages 98 to 100 to assist you with this.

1. If you are going to use the dowsing rods, construct a circular chart similar to that at the top of page 98. Draw it on a sheet of plain, white paper, at least one foot in diameter. Instead of writing the names of the colors on the chart, you may wish to color in each section of the chart itself. If you choose to use the pendulum, draw the sample chart found at the bottom of page 98. Color in the squares for the colors.

2. Take a moment to relax and place both feet flat on the floor. Rest your elbows on the flat surface upon which lays the chart. For the dowsing rod determination, you will only use one of the rods. Hold the rod far enough away from you so that the tip of the rod will not touch any part of you. It should be free to swing in a complete circle. Hold the rod lightly so that your hand is above the center of the circle. At this point, focus on the person whose aura you are reading or upon yourself. If you are reading your own aura, close your eyes and think about yourself.

3. At this point ask yourself some questions. Do this at least mentally, but you may also wish to do it out loud: "What is the primary color of _____'s aura?" Pause and allow the rod to swing and point out the area of the chart that most depicts the color. You may also wish to ask questions about secondary

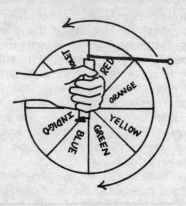

**Using the Dowsing Rods
to Determine the Color of the Aura**

**Using the Pendulum to Determine
the Color of the Aura**

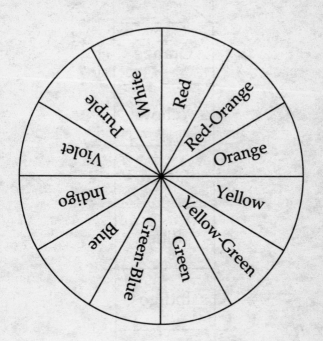

Sample Color Wheel for Dowsing the Aura

Red
Orange
Yellow
Green
Blue
Indigo
Violet
White

**Sample Color Chart for Using the
Pendulum to Determine Aura Colors**

colors: "What is the next most important color in _____'s aura?" If the rod points to an area between two colors, reflect upon the significance of both. Remember there are many shades of color, and they might not all be depicted upon the chart. You may have to use the question: "What color is closest to the color of _____'s aura?"

4. For the chart with the pendulum, the process is the same. Rest your elbow on the flat surface so that the pendulum hangs three to six inches over the chart of colors as depicted on page 100. Start at one end of the chart and work your way through all of the colors.

You will use "yes" and "no" responses of the pendulum to determine the auric colors. Again ask your questions: "Is red a part of _____'s aura?", "Is red the primary color of _____'s aura?" etc. Pay attention to how the pendulum responds. Let it give you its "yes" or "no" answers. Also pay attention to how strongly it responds. The stronger it answers, the stronger that color may be in the aura.

5. Go through each color on the chart with your pendulum. Again, remember you must phrase the question so it can be answered with a "yes" or "no" response. You can even use this to help you locate where these colors are in the aura:

- "Is this red primarily above the head?"
- "Is this green indicating something about the physical body?"
- "Is the blue a dark blue?"
- "Is the yellow located above or below the head in the aura?"

Do not be afraid to experiment. The more you use these tools, the more you become consciously aware that your energies extend beyond physical boundaries. You enhance your perception and break down barriers that can hinder your actual physical senses.

Seeing and Interpreting the Health Aura

When you begin to see the aura, it is usually the area closest to the physical body. This particular area reflects the physical health of the individual to a great degree. In a healthy person, the energy of the physical body appears in the aura as radiant lines of energy. This energy can be of various colors, but it often appears, not like a cloud enveloping the body, but rather more like streams of energy radiating outward from it (refer to the diagram on the next page). They often stand out against the backdrop of the entire auric field.

The appearance of this radiation tells much about the health of the individual. The stronger, more balanced and symmetrical the radiations, the stronger and healthier the individual will be. If there is a lack of symmetry in the radiant lines of energy, then it indicates a weakness, imbalance or dis-ease somewhere within the physical body. The areas of asymmetrical streams can provide clues to the part of the body that is having problems.

It is not unusual to find that imbalances within these physical radiations appear in the aura before the actual illness or physical problem manifests or makes itself known. If you pay attention to the auric field and changes within it, you can take appropriate preventative measures. You can correct the problem before it manifests in a physical illness or discomfort.

In a healthy person, these radiant lines of energy are balanced and strong. They extend from a foot to two feet around the physical body. At that point they begin to fade and blend with the rest of the auric field. If these radiant lines appear balanced and symmetrical but only extend four to eight inches, it can indicate that the person's physical energy is way down. Unless measures are taken to regain the energy, physical problems can eventually result.

Distortions in these radiant lines can indicate

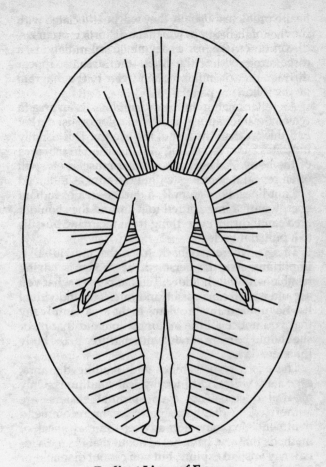

Radiant Lines of Energy

In a healthy person, the energy closest to the physical body will often appear as radiant streams of energy extending one to two feet out into the auric field. They will seem to stand out against the backdrop of the entire auric field. These streams are symmetrical and fine in their radiations.

health problems. Usually they will be associated with the area of the body in which the distortion occurs. A distortion can appear as asymmetrical radiations, a discoloring within the lines (the streams appear dirty) and even inflammation (refer to the diagram on the following page).

An inflammation in the radiant lines is an area in which the lines appear redder in color or just darker and thicker than the rest of the energy. This usually indicates a corresponding inflammation in that area of the body. Aches, pains, pulled muscles etc. will often reveal themselves within the aura as inflamed radiant lines. For example, a darker area of radiant energy with a tinge of red to it around the shoulder area can indicate everything from recurring bursitis to a pulled muscle.

This is where feedback from the individual is important. Ask the person if he or she is having trouble with the shoulder. Tell the person what you see and what it can possibly indicate. If the individual has not noticed any problems in the area, simply say that you notice a little inflammation and that he or she should be extra careful with that area of the body for a few days.

There is a responsibility with reading the aura, especially with regard to physical conditions. Only medical doctors—not even spiritual healers—are authorized to diagnose, prescribe or recommend treatment. You may offer advice; you may speak of methods that you have heard about that the individual may wish to explore, but you cannot diagnose or prescribe!

I have seen instances where, as an individual begins to see the aura, especially the physical aspects reflected within it, they generalize. They see a dark spot in the aura and they tell the individual that there is a cancerous condition or a precancerous state forming. Such conclusions are not only irresponsible, they

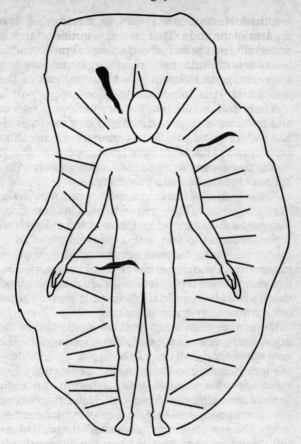

Health Problems Within the Aura

The radiant lines can indicate specific problem areas. The inflammation at the left shoulder and the right hip could reflect pulled or strained muscles. At the head, it could indicate tension and headaches. The asymmetrical radiations can easily reflect poor energy levels, involvement in too many physical activities, poor circulation and/or other problems.

are cruel. Anyone who comes for a reading is in a vulnerable position. That person is opening himself or herself up to be influenced on some very dynamic levels. It is important not to sow negative seeds. It is important not to intrude upon the free will of the individual. It is important to choose your words carefully and considerately. You should be sensitive and intuitive enough to determine how the individual will respond and adjust your communication accordingly. That takes time and proper training. If you cannot do so, then you have no business reading the aura for another as a professional.

These guidelines to colors and appearances in the aura are just that. They are not written in stone. Each individual must be read and interpreted uniquely. If a person comes to you with a problem, physical or otherwise, and you read something of a negative nature into it, you do not have the right to get specific. Say that you see a problem in a particular area, and that it would be beneficial to confirm it one way or the other through a regular physician.

Remember that, when you are dealing with the aura, there are many variables to consider. The colors, the shades of colors, the depth, the vibrancy, the location, the combinations etc. all interplay and influence what you are able to discern. An auric assessment helps you to pinpoint problem areas and give you a good sense of the nature of the imbalances, if any. Discuss your impressions with the individual, but do not make claims that you cannot personally verify. In this way you serve as an educational tool for the other individual. You assist the individual in looking at himself or herself from a different perspective. You awaken the person to a higher awareness of his or her energy essence and help the individual to align with the higher forces of life.

6

Strengthening and Protecting the Aura

At some point in your evolution, you come to the realization that you are made of more than just the physical body. You begin to understand that there is more to the world than meets the eye. Most people focus their concentration upon things that are visible and tangible, but science is proving that we are affected by many things which are not in the least visible to the human eye.

If you are unaware of how extraneous forces can affect you, you can end up with weaknesses in your own energy system. These weaknesses may manifest as actual physical illnesses or as mental/emotional imbalances. Your individual energy system is imposed and impinged upon every day. Unless you learn to recognize this phenomenon and work to protect yourself from unwanted intrusions, you may find your life becoming more complicated.

We have all had experiences in which our energies were affected by outside forces. Extraneous sounds, heat and electrical impositions occur frequently. Other individuals impinge upon your energies as well. Has anyone ever made you feel that you were inferior or a failure? Have you ever been influenced to purchase something or participate in an activity when you really did not want to? Have you ever felt drained after talking with some individual?

All of these are intrusions upon your energy field.

The key to protecting your energies lies with the aura. With a strong and vibrant aura, negative, draining and unbalanced energies are deflected. Maintaining such an aura is not difficult. Most beneficial to the aura are positive health practices. Proper diet, exercise and fresh air are strengthening to the entire auric field. On the other hand, lack of exercise, lack of fresh air, improper diet, abuse of alcohol, drugs, tobacco etc. create wear and tear upon the fabric of the aura.

The aura is also extremely affected by emotional and mental states—more than most people realize. Continued stress, emotional trauma, mental disorders or imbalances, upheavals, worry, fear and other negative emotions and attitudes weaken the auric field. A weakened aura results in energy drains. You become tired more easily. If prolonged, holes and tears can occur within the fabric of the auric field. Physical health problems will begin to manifest, along with other imbalances. The diagram on the next page shows how a weakened aura can appear. It has holes, dark areas and an unbalanced, weak form.

There are many simple ways of vitalizing and strengthening the human aura. Sunlight is strengthening to the auric field. So is physical exercise. Fresh air is extremely vitalizing to the aura. Eating less food, but more frequently, has a more balanced effect upon the aura. Keeping the bowels clean assists in keeping the aura strong and resilient. Meditation is also strengthening and protective. You do not have to become excessive in these practices. Moderation in all things is beneficial to keeping the aura vibrant.

Music can also be used to balance and strengthen the auric field. Gregorian chants are very cleansing to negative energies in the aura or within the environment. We have all had experiences when we walked into a room in which there had been a fight or argu-

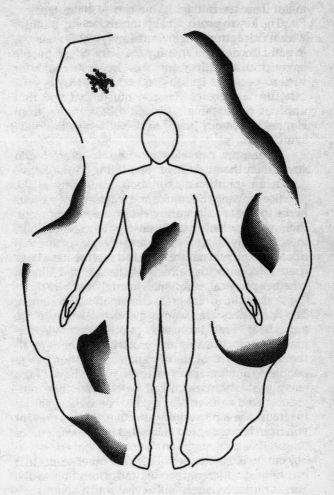

The Appearance of
a Weakened and Unbalanced Aura

ment. The air is thick. You can feel the tension. Playing a Gregorian Chant for about ten minutes within the room can cleanse it of any negative energy. It will also do the same for the aura. Some people have difficulty with the music of Gregorian chants for various personal reasons and tastes. If that is your case, use a piece of classical music that you find uplifting or soothing. This could be anything from Handel's "Water Music" to Beethoven's "Pastoral" symphony.

Fragrances can also be used to protect and strengthen the auric field. Smudging in the native American tradition is common. Smudging is the practice of using the smoke and fragrance of various herbs to cleanse the auric field or the environment. Fragrances, whether as incense or as essential oils, most strongly affect the aura and energies of an emotional and mental nature. Oils and incense have been used to counter the effects of disease and illness, whether physical, emotional, mental or spiritual.

A sage and sweet-grass combination is common. The fragrances are cleansing and balancing to the auric field. Frankincense is another common fragrance that is cleansing and protecting to the aura, although, because of its Christian association, some people do not find it so. However, it does have a high energy vibration which can be effective. For individuals who work in healing and counseling, gardenia fragrance is powerfully effective. It helps prevent you from becoming too entangled in the problems of others. It helps strengthen the aura so that emotional objectivity is maintained. There are other scents that can be just as strengthening and protecting to the aura. A little research will reveal much about their dynamic effects.

Another tool for protecting and strengthening the aura is a quartz crystal or stone. The electrical energy inherent within a crystal will amplify and strengthen the auric field. A good experiment to prove this is to have someone measure your aura *without* a crystal in your hand and then *with* one in your hand. Even a small, one-inch quartz crystal will increase the auric field by as much as three to four feet.

Double-terminated quartz crystals (points on both ends) are extremely effective for strengthening the aura. Carrying one in your pocket can stabilize the aura. This is effective especially if you know you will be going into tense or draining situations. It helps prevent you from being overly taxed and tired.

At the end of the day, when you find yourself drained or just wishing to regain your energy levels, sit or stand with a double-terminated quartz crystal in both hands (refer to the diagram on the next page). Relax and visualize the energy of the crystal recharging your body and filling your auric field with energy. Perform rhythmic breathing to assist this. Five to ten minutes is all that it takes to balance out your energies and strengthen them. This also helps you to shift from a work state of mind to a more relaxed, home state of mind. It helps you to leave the office stuff behind, for it cleanses the aura of energy debris you carried out of the office with you.

The exercises that follow are beneficial for protecting and strengthening the entire auric field. They help balance and energize you. They also help prevent intrusion from unwanted forces and energies. The stronger and more vibrant you keep the aura, the less you will have your energies intruded upon.

TECHNIQUE #1: PREVENTING YOURSELF FROM BEING DRAINED

We have all experienced being drained by another person. You may talk to him or her on the

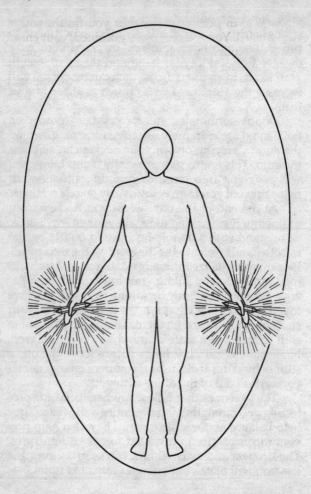

The Effects of Crystals on the Auric Field
Double-terminated quartz crystals stabilize the energy
field around the body and rebuild it. They strengthen
and supplement your normal energy levels.

phone or in person, and, when you finish, you are exhausted. You feel completely drained, your energy is gone, your stomach may ache etc. What you are experiencing is an energy drain.

Some individuals draw or suck off the energy of others. Most of the time this happens because the individuals involved do not realize it. In many cases they are using your energies to *supplement* their own rather than *building up* their own. All they may realize is that, when they finish talking with you or being with you, they feel better. This does not give them a right to take your energy, however, and you should not allow it.

This does not mean that you should accuse this person of being a vampire or say that you will not speak to him or her again because he or she is sucking off your energy. If you do, this person will think you have gone off the deep end. In that case, your problem will be solved, because he or she will probably not care to see you after that. Most people still are not open to the subtle aspects of energy, and you must keep this in mind when dealing with them.

It is easier just to correct the situation without saying a word about it. You can control whether another shares your energy or not. One of the simplest methods is to close your circuit of energy. There are currents of energy flowing through your body and around it within the auric field. You can close them down so that your energies only circulate around your own auric field and throughout your body. You prevent your energies from being drawn off from the aura, and you prevent your aura from drawing in another's energy.

Assuming the posture shown on the next page is all it takes. You cross your feet at the ankles and bring your thumbs and fingers together so they are touching. (If you wish, you can use just your thumbs and

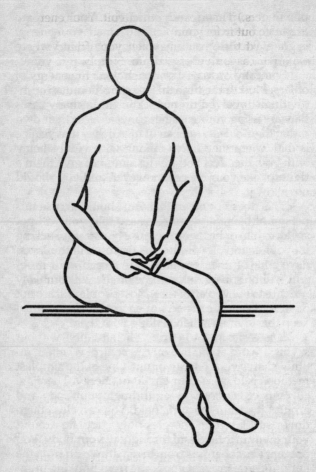

Preventing Yourself from Being Drained
This posture closes off the circuit of your energy.
Touching thumbs and index fingers or thumbs and all
fingers, while legs are crossed at ankles, stops your
energy from being sucked off by another.

index fingers.) This closes your circuit. Your energy will not go out from you.

The next time you encounter your friend who drains you, assume this posture. Simply rest your hands casually on your lap, touch your fingers and cross your ankles. It is casual and simple, and no one will suspect you of anything. You can also do this when on the phone with such people.

If you do this, you will get some feedback through other friends as to the effects. You may hear comments such as, "You are just not as nice," "You are not as open as you used to be," "I wonder if so-and-so is mad at me" etc. It has nothing to do with being mad at people. You will still be talking with them as nicely and as often as ever. What you are not doing is allowing them to take your energy! You simply are not allowing them to drain you. Because they are not getting "high" from you, they are assuming something is wrong. No one has the right to take your energy without your permission.

TECHNIQUE #2
ENERGY BREATHING TECHNIQUE

Fresh air and proper breathing are essential to a strong and vital aura. Breathing for maximum energy to the aura should be done through the nostrils. Many people have a bad habit of mouth breathing, not realizing that nostril breathing is more natural and healthy.

Mouth breathing makes an individual more susceptible to diseases. It impairs the vitality of the aura. It can even weaken the constitution. Between the mouth and the lungs, there is nothing to strain the air. Dust, dirt and other impure substances have a clear track to the lungs. Mouth breathing also admits cold air to the lungs, which can lead to inflammation of the respiratory organs.

Nostril breathing, on the other hand, is more vitalizing and healthy to your entire energy system. The nose provides specialized surfaces for the absorption of *prana* from the air. Prana can be likened to the vitalizing aspect that exists within air. Many Eastern breathing techniques require a conscious focus upon the tip of the nose and the entire nasal area during inhalation. This enhances the prana absorption, raises the vitality of the entire aura and stimulates the entire energy system of the human being.

The nostrils and the nasal passages are designed with hair to filter and sieve the air. They also warm the air through the mucous membranes. This makes the air fit for the delicate organs of the lungs, and breath is then more energizing and strengthening to your auric field.

In yoga, the moon breath is termed the *Ida* and the sun breath is termed the *Pingala*. The balance of the two is *Susumna*. Your energy has polarity, positive and negative, male and female, sun and moon. This breathing technique quickly energizes the aura and balances the polarity of the body. It also enhances your ability to remember and assimilate information. It balances the hemispheres of the brain. It can be used before studies to shorten learning time. It can also be used as a quick pick-me-up during the day.

The basic technique is comprised of alternate breaths, breathing in one nostril and then breathing out the other. (Remember that conscious attention to the tip of the nose, especially during the in-breath, will magnify the effects of this technique.) The rhythm is aided by holding the nose with the thumb and fingers.

1. Begin with your right thumb and fingers over your nose and exhale. Place your tongue against the roof of your mouth behind your front teeth.

2. Use your thumb and close your right nostril;

then inhale through your left nostril for a slow count of four.

3. Keeping your right nostril closed, clamp your fingers down over your left nostril, pinching your nose closed between your thumb and fingers. Hold for a count of 16. (If you have never performed any concentrated rhythmic breathing, the count of 16 may be too long for you. If this is the case, reduce it or count faster. With practice, you will develop the ability to hold your breath for more extended periods. Try inhaling for a count of three, holding for a count of six and then exhaling for a count of three. Work to find the rhythm that is most effective for you and then build upon it.)

4. Release your thumb, opening your right nostril. Keep your left nostril closed with your fingers. Exhale slowly out through your right nostril for a count of eight.

5. Release your nose, raise your left hand up and, with your thumb, close off your left nostril. Inhale for a count of four through your right nostril and then clamp your fingers closed on it. Hold for a count of 16.

6. Release your thumb and your left nostril. Keep your right nostril clamped with your fingers. Exhale for a slow count of eight through your left nostril.

7. Repeat four to five breaths, alternating each side. Breathe in one nostril, hold and exhale out the other. Reverse it and repeat the procedure. Do at least four to five breaths for each side for a quick pick-me-up. This will saturate your entire body and aura with quick energy.

TECHNIQUE #3
THE CLEANSING VORTEX

This exercise is a visualization exercise for cleansing and purifying your entire auric field. It is an excellent exercise to perform at the end of a day, especially at those times when you have interacted with a great many people. It helps sweep out energy debris, preventing it from accumulating and creating imbalance within the auric field. It only takes about five minutes to be effective.

1. Take a seated position and perform a progressive relaxation. Performing the breathing technique just described is beneficial as a preparation for this exercise. You may want to use a simple prayer or mantra as well. Remember that the exercise as presented here is a guideline, and you should learn to adapt it to your own energies.

2. About 20 feet above you, in your mind's eye, visualize a small whirlwind of crystalline white fire beginning to form. It looks like a small, spiritual tornado. As it forms its funnel shape, visualize it so that it is large enough to encompass your entire auric field. The small end of the funnel should be visualized as capable of entering through the crown of your head and passing down the middle pillar of your body (see the diagram on page 120).

3. This whirlwind of spiritual fire should be seen as rotating and spinning clockwise. As it touches your aura, see it as sucking up and burning off all of the energy debris you have accumulated.

4. See, feel and imagine it moving down, over and through your entire aura and body. Know that it is sweeping your energy field clean of all the extraneous energies you have accumulated throughout the day.

5. As it moves through your body, allow this energy vortex to exit out through your feet down into the heart of the earth itself. See the vortex as carrying this energy debris into the lower realms, where it is used to fertilize and benefit the lower kingdoms of life upon and within the planet.

TECHNIQUE #4
THE MIDDLE PILLAR EXERCISE

This exercise is drawn from an ancient system of development known as the mystical Qabala. It employs sound, visualization and breathing to pump the aura with tremendous amounts of energy. It helps seal leaks and holes within the auric field. It stabilizes and balances the aura. It increases your energy levels so that you have greater amounts with which to carry out your daily tasks. It prevents your energies from being overtapped.

The exercise involves using ancient Hebrew names for God, like mantras, in conjunction with specific images and breathing. This combination creates what is called a synergistic effect. It does not make it three times as strong but actually eight times as strong. The three aspects of it (the names, the imaging and the breathing) increase the energy exponentially (in this case, two to the third power).

1. Assume a sitting or standing position. Take a few moments and relax.

2. Visualize a crystalline white sphere of light gently coming toward you from the heavens until it is just over your head. It is vibrant and alive with energy. As you vibrate the following name, see and feel this light growing with intensity and filling the entire head region of your body.

3. Softly sound the name EHEIEH *(Eh-huh-yeh)*. Emphasize each syllable, feeling the crown of your head come alive with energy. Repeat this name five to ten times. This name translates as "I AM THAT I AM."

4. Pause, and visualize a shaft of light descending from this sphere, pouring down toward the throat area of your body where a second sphere of light forms. As you vibrate out loud the God-Name, YHVH ELOHIM *(Yah-hoh-vah-Eh-loh-heem)*, this

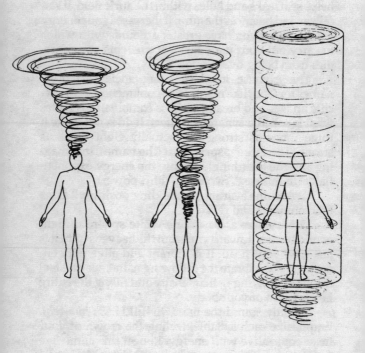

Creating the Cleansing Vortex

sphere of light grows more vibrant and brilliant. Vibrate this name five to ten times. This name means "The Lord God of Creation."

5. Pause and visualize a shaft of light descending from this sphere down to the heart area of the body. Here a third sphere of brilliant light forms. Slowly, syllable by syllable, vibrate the God-name YHVH ELOAH VaDAATH *(Yah-hoh-vah-Eh-loh-ah-Vuh-Dahht)*. Repeat this five to ten times, feeling the sphere of light grow stronger and filling that part of your body. This name means "God made manifest in the mind."

6. Pause and visualize a shaft of light descending from this sphere of light down to the area of your groin. See and feel a fourth sphere of light form itself with brilliance. Vibrate the God-Name SHADDAI EL CHAI *(Shah-dye-El-Keye)* slowly five to ten times. Feel the energy coming alive within this area of the body. This name means "the Almighty Living God."

7. Pause and visualize the shaft of light descending from this fourth sphere of light down to the area of your feet. Here a fifth sphere forms, while the shaft descends down into the heart of the earth itself. As you vibrate the sound of the God-name ADONAI HaARETZ *(Ah-doh-nye-Hah-Ah-retz)*, the sphere grows with crystalline brilliance. Repeat this five to ten times. This name means "Lord of the Earth."

8. You have now formed the Middle Pillar of balance through your entire body and aura. Bring your attention back to the crown of your head and begin rhythmic breathing. As you exhale slowly to a count of four, see and feel energy pour down the left side of your body, radiating outward, strengthening your aura on that side of your body. Inhale for a count of four and draw energy up the right side of your body from your feet to the crown of your head. See and feel this energy radiating outward, strengthening your

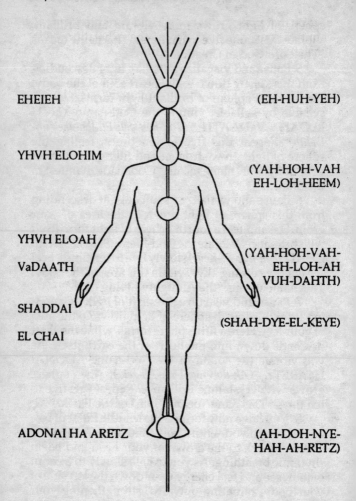

EHEIEH (EH-HUH-YEH)

YHVH ELOHIM (YAH-HOH-VAH
EH-LOH-HEEM)

YHVH ELOAH (YAH-HOH-VAH-
VaDAATH EH-LOH-AH
VUH-DAHTH)

SHADDAI (SHAH-DYE-EL-KEYE)

EL CHAI

ADONAI HA ARETZ (AH-DOH-NYE-
HAH-AH-RETZ)

The Middle Pillar Exercise

aura on that side of your body. Hold your breath for a count of four, and then repeat the exhalation and inhalation. Do this four to five times.

9. Now, as you exhale, see and feel the energy stream down the front of your body for a count of four. Inhale, and allow it to stream up the back. Hold for a count of four and repeat four to five times. You have now strengthened your entire auric field. Feel this energy surrounding you. Know that it has sealed any leaks. Know that it has replaced any lost energy.

10. Now feel the energy gathering at your feet. As you inhale, draw rainbow-colored light up through your feet, up through that middle pillar to the crown of your head. As you exhale, spray that rainbow light out the top of your head to fill your entire auric field with its color and energy. Pause and allow yourself to bask in this brilliant and renewed energy field.

The Middle Pillar exercise is also cleansing to the entire auric field. It strengthens it and facilitates the development of higher energies, including your own psychic abilities. Because it raises the energy of the individual to such a high level, it also helps in the development of vision of the auric field. It increases overall perception and sensitivity—physical and otherwise.

I teach this exercise in my workshops and stress it as absolutely fundamental. It should be employed by anyone wishing to open up his or her higher faculties. It is so powerful and so effective that it should become the staple of those just beginning as well as those who have involved themselves in the metaphysical field for years. It is grounding, protective and strengthening. I have not found a single exercise that can do so much and adapt itself so much to the individual.

Traditionally with the Middle Pillar exercise, five spheres of light are used. A dynamic variation is to incorporate a sixth. This sixth sphere of light is activated in the area of the third eye or the brow center. This chakra center is linked to physical vision as well as psychic vision (clairvoyance). This particular variation is even more dynamic in stimulating auric vision.

1. Begin as before in a sitting position. Close your eyes and relax.

2. Visualize the crystalline ball of light descending from the heavens to come to rest at the crown of your head. As you vibrate the name EHEIEH (Eh-huh-yeh), feel the crown of your head come alive with energy. Repeat five to ten times.

3. Visualize a shaft of light descending from this sphere to form a second sphere in the area of your brow. Intone the god-name JEHOVAH (Yah-hoh-vah) softly. Visualize the sound carrying to the ends of the universe and back. Feel your inner eyes coming alive with energy. Repeat five to ten times.

4. From this sphere, the shaft of light descends further to form a third sphere of light in the area of your throat. Vibrate the God-name JEHOVAH ELOHIM (Yah-hoh-vah-Eh-loh-heem). See and feel this sphere of light come to life with brilliant vibrancy. Repeat five to ten times.

5. From this sphere, the shaft descends and forms a fourth sphere of light in the area of your heart. It comes alive with each intonation of the God-name JEHOVAH ALOAH VaDAATH (Yah-hoh-vah-Eh-loh-ah-Vuh-Dahth). Repeat five to ten times.

6. Pause and visualize the shaft of light descending from the heart sphere to the area of your groin. There, a fifth sphere of light forms. See it form and radiate brilliance with each intonation of the God-name SHADDAI EL CHAI (Shah-dye-El-Kye).

7. Again pause, and then visualize the shaft of light descending from this fifth sphere down to your feet. Here a sixth sphere of light forms, and the shaft

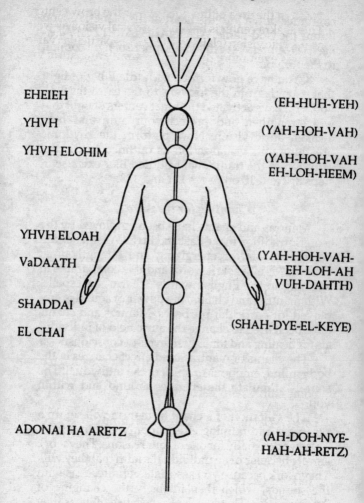

EHEIEH

YHVH

YHVH ELOHIM

YHVH ELOAH

VaDAATH

SHADDAI

EL CHAI

ADONAI HA ARETZ

(EH-HUH-YEH)

(YAH-HOH-VAH)

(YAH-HOH-VAH
EH-LOH-HEEM)

(YAH-HOH-VAH-
EH-LOH-AH
VUH-DAHTH)

(SHAH-DYE-EL-KEYE)

(AH-DOH-NYE-
HAH-AH-RETZ)

Variation on the Middle Pillar

continues down into the heart of the planet. As you intone the God-name, ADONAI HaARETZ *(Ah-doh-nye-Hah-Ah-retz)*, see this sixth sphere of light coming to life for you.

8. You have now formed a Middle Pillar of light that extends from the heavens to the earth through you. You have activated the inner centers of light that will strengthen and protect your aura and help awaken auric vision. Now perform the rhythmic breathing and visualization as outlined in the description of the traditional Middle Pillar exercise in steps 8, 9 and 10 on pages 121 and 123.

Chanting for the Aura

Mantras and chants have been employed by the esoteric tradition in the East and in the West. They are powerful tools for energizing and strengthening. "Mantra" is a Sanskrit word, and it is comparable in meaning to the English words "charm" or "spell." With mantras and chants, the power of sound is employed for particular purposes. Mantras and chants have been used to change the auric field of individuals for healing and for higher levels of consciousness.

The chants or mantras used effect changes in the body, mind, emotions or spirit of the individual. The sounds stimulate the energies around and within you.

The vibration of a chant or mantra will set up a purifying and refining effect upon your auric field. They work usually for one of four reasons. They work simply because of an individual's faith that they will. They work because you associate definite ideas with the sounds, which then intensify the changing of your energies. They work also because of what they do mean. The meaning beats upon your mental body, resulting in an impression being formulated within your energy patterns. Many mantras and chants work because of their sounds alone, regardless of meaning. The sounds impinge upon the auric field, creating changes in it.

Chanting is the process that releases energy that makes the recital of mystical words and sounds mysterious and powerful. The rhythm of the chanting is critical. Chanted mantras have dynamic effects. How many times to chant a mantra before it takes effect is often debated. As in most things, you must decide what works best for you. Ten to 15 minutes of a particular chant is usually enough to experience its effects.

Working with chants and mantras is simple. Choose a mantra and familiarize yourself with the significance if you can. Choose a time in which you will not be disturbed and allow yourself to relax. Begin chanting, syllable by syllable. Allow the mantra to find its own rhythm, one that is comfortable for you.

When you stop, you should still hear the mantra echoing within your mind. There may even be a slight buzzing in the ears. These are signals that it has effected an energy change. Don't be upset if you don't experience these things. It doesn't mean the mantra has not worked for you. They are simply guidelines.

As you listen to the mantra echoing in your mind, meditate upon the energies associated with that mantra. See them active within your entire auric field. Focus on how much more light and energy has been awakened within and around you. See your aura touching others with greater vibrancy.

Sample Mantras

1. *OM*

Om is considered the most powerful mantra of all. It corresponds to the Egyptian *Amen* and actually represents the name of the divine Logos. *Om* is the Sanskrit word for the spark of life itself, that part of the divine imprisoned within physical life.

It is believed by many that there are several hundred ways of pronouncing and intoning *Om*—each with its own unique effect upon the aura. When you emphasize and prolong the "O," you affect others and your own auric field. When the "M" (humming sound) is prolonged, the entire effect is produced more internally.

When you sound the *Om*, you need to see yourself rising from the domination of physical life. You need to visualize your limiting and hindering thought-forms as being shattered. You need to see the energy debris you have accumulated within the aura being cleansed. *Om* is the sound of contact with the divine, and thus it is an instrument for freeing your energies. It has the power to cleanse, create and release the new so that you can move on to higher expressions of energy.

Om is also a call to attention. It settles and stabilizes the auric field. It arranges the particles of your subtle bodies into alignment. *All* of your energy responds to this sound. When these energies are aligned, you can more easily restore health and gain greater benefit through meditation.

A variation of *Om* is *AUM (Ah-oh-mm)*. This form enhances your visualization of the aura, and it enables your thoughts to become more crystallized. It is an affirmation that your energies are at their highest and continually growing higher, as if you are saying to yourself on a primal level: "So let it be!" *Aum* also helps repair weaknesses and holes within your auric field.

A good visualization to perform with the chanting of *Om* is to envision the Sanskrit letters for *Om* overlaying your physical body (see the diagram on

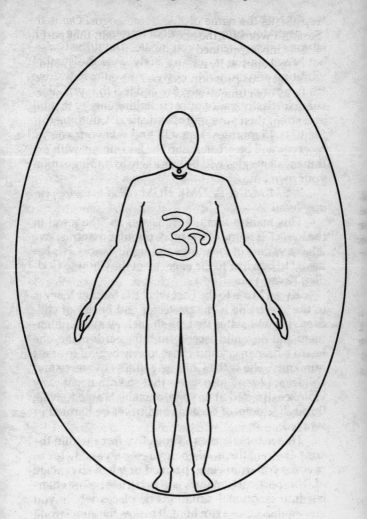

Using the Sanskrit *Om* to Strengthen the Aura

the preceding page).

Begin by seeing the symbol forming in the trunk of your body. Then, as you inhale, sound the *Om* silently within the mind and body. Feel the symbol vibrating and gathering power. As you exhale, tone the *Om* outward, audibly. See and feel the symbol issuing forth streams of pure crystalline energy that fill and strengthen your entire auric field. Continue this for 10 to 15 minutes. You will find that your energy reserves will be greater, and the encounters with extraneous energies will be less likely to impinge upon your own aura.

2. *OM MANI PADME HUM (Ohm-mah-nee-pod-may-hum)*

This mantra literally translates as "the jewel in the lotus." It is one of the more popular mantras, and it has a variety of meanings and significances. It is believed to be a link to the energies of the Chinese Goddess Kwan Yin.

Kwan Yin is to the East what the Mother Mary is to the West. She is the protector and healer of children. Legend states that, as she achieved enlightenment and began to ascend from the earth plane, she heard a human cry and chose to stay behind to assist humanity. She is the Chinese goddess of mercy and children. Legend also states that she can negate any violence directed at anyone, and she is able to walk through legions of demons and never be harmed or swayed.

This mantra acts as a protective force within the aura. It strengthens all energy reserves and helps to prevent you from being drained or taken advantage of. This particular mantra is good to use before entering into emotional situations or places where you know tensions can run high. It makes the aura strong enough to prevent others from intruding upon you, physically or otherwise.

The six syllables of the mantra activate energies for transforming the debris within your aura into a purified force. It balances emotions and assists in healing the body.

OM—This is the totality of existence and of sound. It is the call signal. Through resonating this part of the mantra, you can set up a link between your auric field and that of the one called Kwan Yin.

MANI— This literally means "jewel." It refers to a kind of non-substance that is impervious to harm or change. It is a symbol of the highest value within the mind. It symbolizes enlightenment with compassion and love. Just as a jewel can remove poverty, this aspect of the mantra helps to remove discordant energies from your aura.

PADME—Literally, this translates as "lotus." It is a symbol of spiritual unfoldment and the awakening of finer energies within your auric field. It has a sound that helps to clarify the energy debris muddying your own aura. It helps you to sort it out and assimilate its corresponding circumstances. It harmonizes your aura.

HUM—This sound is untranslatable, *per se*. While *Om* represents the infinite sound within you and the universe, *Hum* represents the finite within the infinite. It stands for the potential of the auric field. It awakens your sensitivity to energies around you, and it increases your awareness of how they are affecting you. It awakens your perception of the physical aura and stimulates harmony within it so that you can understand yourself more effectively as an energy system.

As in the first mantra, relax. Close your eyes and, as you inhale, sound the mantra silently to yourself. As you then exhale, sound it audibly, projecting it outward, syllable by syllable. Find your own rhythm. Let it work for you. Know that, as you use it, your aura will become stronger and more protected at all times.

The Golden Wedding Garment

The "Golden Wedding Garment" is a phrase that has come down to us through esoteric Christianity. The ancient initiation ceremonies were not open to any and all people, as some may assume, but only to those who were qualified. This is reflected in the Christian parable of the king's supper (Matthew 22:2-14). No one could enter who was not arrayed in the golden wedding garment. This garment is the purified aura and soul of the individual.

This purified aura occurs through sublimating the lower desires and living a life of selfless service and love to all humanity and to every living creature. This garment surrounding the body is comprised of the energy colors of blue and gold. It is the aura and soul of the individual that, when strengthened and purified, will enable him or her to become a true *invisible helper*, one who can consciously use this body to visit other people and places while awake or asleep.

For the aura to become this dynamic and purified, the chakra centers need to be more fully activated and cleansed as well. These chakra centers were discussed previously in Chapter 2. They have been described as centers of light within the body. In the East, they were referred to as lotus flowers and, in esoteric Christianity, they are often referred to as the roses of light. When these roses of light mediate purified energy in and around the body, the aura becomes like a golden wedding garment.

The meditation that follows is a dynamic exercise for activating 12 of these centers of light. Traditionally, people focus upon seven of the chakra centers. The 12 centers within this exercise are more energizing and balancing to the aura than just focusing upon the traditional seven. These 12 centers are latent within every person. When awakened and fully functioning, they become 12 glorious body lights that infuse the aura with a golden radiance (see the diagram on the next page).

These 12 roses of light are symbolic to a great degree. The number 12 has had much symbolism attached to it in the past, the most obvious being the 12 signs of the zodiac.

The roses of light within your feet are awakened through dedicating your life to service and by walking in the steps of the ancient masters and never wearying of doing good for others.

The roses of light in your knees are awakened after hours of prayer and meditation and when humility becomes both an attribute and a keynote of your life. The roses of light within your hands are awakened when you apply yourself to the service of others, extending your hands to help and to heal. They become more vibrant as you strive to learn and perform something new each day.

The rose at the base of your spine—the area of the traditional base chakra—is more fully awakened as you increasingly purify your energies and learn to transmute the lower.

The rose of light in the area of your solar plexus is actually a joining of the two traditional chakra centers at the spleen and solar plexus. As the mind and emotions are balanced, they come together as a new source of light.

The rose in your heart shines forth as compassion encompasses all life that you encounter. As you learn to love with proper compassion and knowledge, it shines forth to heal you and others within your life.

The rose within your throat awakens fully when you learn to use the power of the word. As long as there are hasty, unkind or destructive words, this

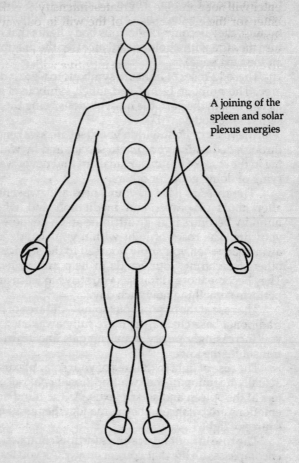

A joining of the spleen and solar plexus energies

**The 12 Chakras of the Modern Disciple
and Initiate**
These 12 lights are latent within the body of *every* person.
They are 12 energy centers which, when awakened and
functioning, become the 12 glorious body lights!

center will not unfold to its greatest intensity. It is the center for the creative force of the will in outward expression.

The rose of light within your brow center comes alive when you can balance the intuitive with the intellectual. As you develop trust in your inner sight and awaken your innate feminine energies of nurturing, imagination and intuition, it will give birth to greater auric illumination.

The rose of light at the crown of your head is the seat of your masculine energies. As you learn to assert the feminine energies of nurturing and illumination and act upon them within your own life circumstances, this center begins to shine forth.

The following meditation is designed to help awaken these centers of light and illuminate the aura. It is an effective exercise to perform on a regular basis. I recommend performing it at least once per month. For this exercise, make sure that you will be undisturbed. Take the phone off of the hook and make yourself comfortable. You may wish to perform a progressive relaxation, sending warm and soothing feelings to different parts of your body. Use slow rhythmic breathing to assist you. Breathe deeply and relax. As you begin to relax, allow your energies to gather around you. Imagine that someone has just placed an old comfortable quilt about your shoulders. You are warm, safe and at peace.

As you begin to relax, you see yourself at the top of a stairwell. At the bottom is a faint, soft light that entices and invites you down. With each step down, you relax more and more deeply. You feel yourself growing lighter and lighter. As you reach the halfway point on the stairs, you are so weightless that your feet barely touch the stairs themselves. Still you go down, and it feels wonderful. You had forgotten how nice it was to relax and allow yourself to simply float.

At the bottom of the stairs, you find yourself in a small circular room. In the center of the room is a tall, ornate mirror. The soft light that drew you down the stairs rests above the mirror. You move from the staircase to stand before the mirror. At first there is no image, and then, as you stare into it, there is a soft fluttering, and you see before you an image of yourself.

You are naked, and you see yourself in your ideal form. You see yourself as the true inner you. It warms you and heals you. You realize that you had begun to forget just how beautiful you are.

As you look into the mirror, you see two small rose buds forming on top of your feet. Soft and beautiful, they begin to unfold, petal by petal. As they unfold, you remember all of the steps you have taken in this life to get you where you are today. You remember the wrong turns you have taken, and you remember the times your steps were smooth and easy. You see the times when others helped direct your steps. And then you see the path of light that lies ahead of you, the promise of the future.

Next you see roses beginning to form upon your knees. They are just as soft and beautiful as those upon your feet. As the petals unfold before your eyes, you remember the times when others knelt to help you. You remember the times you have fallen and had to pick yourself up. You remember the times when you saw others fall and you stopped, knelt and assisted them in some way.

As you look into the mirror, you see roses forming within the palms of your hands. Soft and vibrant, they too unfold petal by petal. As they do, images of the past pass before your eyes. You remember the times when others may have raised a hand to you in anger, and you remember the times when a loving hand helped wipe away the tears. You remember when others extended their hands in friendship and assistance, and you see the times when you extended yours to others. You see the people in your life that are blessed by the soft touch of your hand upon their cheek in love.

Next you see a rose form in the area of your groin. As it unfolds before your eyes, you see those aspects of your life that you have cleansed and purified. You see the areas of your life that you have changed to your own benefit. You also see those areas still needing further work and effort.

Yet another rose appears in the area just below your solar plexus. As it unfolds before your eyes, you see all the times when your emotions got away from you. You see all the times when you would not let your emotions out. You also begin to see those times when you responded to people and situations with combined concern and action. You see the times when you were effective in swaying others to something positive and wonderful within their lives.

Next a rose appears within your heart, and, as it unfolds, you remember all of the times when you loved and lost. You also remember times when others returned it. You see the love of those who are around you at the moment, and you can see how your ability to love even more in the future will make you a healing force in the lives of those you touch.

A tenth rose now appears in your throat area and unfolds petal by petal. As it does, you remember the times when harsh and discouraging words were spoken to you. You remember the times you said harsh and negative things to others or about others. And then you see those times when someone's words lifted you, thrilled you, encouraged you and strengthened you. You also see those currently around you who could use some kind and encouraging words themselves. You make a mental note to speak to them soon.

The eleventh rose forms in your brow area. As it forms, you remember all of the dreams you had growing up. You remember the times you failed to nurture them. You see the times you refused to follow your higher imaginings. Then you see the dreams that are beginning to unfold for you. They stir your imagination, and you remember that you are never given a hope, wish or dream without also being given an opportunity to make it a reality, and the only thing that can shatter it is compromise.

As the last rose unfolds, the one upon the crown of your head, you see all that you need to do to make your dreams a reality. You see the promise of the future if you will but assert your energies in that direction. This is the rose for the fulfillment of your life.

As the 12 roses stand out upon you, they begin to shine and glow with a renewed radiance. The energy begins to pour out of them. A golden radiance issues forth surrounding you, as if a garment of golden light is being placed about you. As the golden garment fills your entire aura, radiating light and health, you mentally offer a prayer of thanks for this reminder of your true essence.

You make a mental note to keep the roses alive, and as you do the image in the mirror fades. And although the reflection disappears, you still feel upon you the roses, vibrant with light and energy, and you are aware of the brilliant gold surrounding you within your aura.

It is this feeling that stays with you as you turn toward the stairs and ascend to your conscious awareness, bringing with you the promise of the 12 roses of light and the Golden Wedding Garment.

There are many ways of becoming more sensitive to the subtle energy fields of life. Learning to see the aura not only breaks down your old barriers, but it increases your sensitivity. It bridges the physical and the metaphysical. As you develop the ability to see and feel the more subtle aspects of life, you are blessed in other ways. Your intuition unfolds and increases, and the childlike joy and wonder of life returns. Every day becomes a new adventure! Every day becomes a new blessing!

Bibliography

Buckland, Raymond, *Practical Color Magick*. Llewellyn Publications, St. Paul, MN, 1983.

Butler, W.E., *How to Read the Aura*. Aquarian Press, Wellingborough, Northamptonshire, UK, 1979.

Guyton, Arthur, *Basic Human Physiology*. W.B. Saunders, Philadelphia, PA, 1971.

Leadbeater, C.W., *Man—Visible and Invisible*. Theosophical Publishing, London, UK, 1981.

Nielsen, Greg and Polansky, Joseph, *Pendulum Power*. Warner Destiny Books, New York, NY, 1977.

Powell, A.E., *The Etheric Double*. Theosophical Publishing, Wheaton, IL, 1983.

Prophet, Mark, *Studies of the Human Aura*. Summit University Press, Los Angeles, CA, 1975.

Schwarz, Jack, *Human Energy Systems*. E.P. Dutton, New York, NY, 1980.

WIlson, Annie and Bek, Lilla, *What Color Are You?* Turnstone Press, Wellingborough, Northamptonshire, UK, 1981.

Yogi Ramacharaka, *The Science of Breath*. Yogi Publishing Society, Chicago, IL, 1905.

STAY IN TOUCH

On the following pages you will find listed, with their current prices, some of the books now available on related subjects. Your book dealer stocks most of these, and will stock new titles in the Llewellyn series as they become available. We urge your patronage.

To obtain a FREE COPY of our latest full CATALOG of New Age books, tapes, videos, products and services, just write to the address below. In each 80-page catalog sent out bimonthly, you will find articles, reviews, the latest information on New Age topics, a listing of news and events, and much more. It is an exciting and informative way to stay in touch with the New Age and the world. The first copy will be sent free of charge and you will continue receiving copies as long as you are an active customer. You may also subscribe to *The Llewellyn New Times* by sending a $7.00 donation ($20.00 for overseas). Order your copy of *The Llewellyn New Times* today!

The Llewellyn New Times
P.O. Box 64383-Dept. 013, St. Paul, MN 55164

TO ORDER BOOKS AND PRODUCTS ON THE FOLLOWING PAGES:

If your book dealer does not carry the titles listed on the following pages, you may order them directly from Llewellyn. Please send full price in U.S. funds, plus $3.00 for postage and handling for orders *under* $10.00; $4.00 for orders *over* $10.00. There are no postage and handling charges for orders over $50. Postage and handling rates are subject to change. UPS Delivery: We ship UPS whenever possible. Delivery guaranteed. Provide your street address as UPS does not deliver to P.O. Boxes; UPS to Canada requires a $50 minimum order. Allow 4-6 weeks for delivery. Orders outside the USA and Canada: Airmail—add retail price of book; add $5 for each non-book item (tapes, etc.); add $1 per item for surface mail. You may use your major credit card to order these titles by calling 1-800-THE-MOON, M-F, 8:00-5:00, Central Time. Send orders to:

LLEWELLYN PUBLICATIONS
P.O. BOX 64383-013
St. Paul, MN 55164-0383, U.S.A.

THE SACRED POWER IN YOUR NAME
by Ted Andrews

Many seek or wish for some magical incantation that can help them in life, but few realize that, when you are born, you are given your own individual "magickal word." This word can unleash unlimited possibilities within this incarnation. This word is your name.

Learn how family karma is reflected through the surname, the dangers and benefits of changing your name, how to transmute your name into a magickal incantation, how to heal yourself through your name's tones, how to convert your name to music and discover your "name song."

A large portion of this book consists of a metaphysical dictionary of more than 200 names. Each name listing includes its meaning, a suggested affirmation, the vowel elements in the name, the chakra connected with the vowels, and variations on the name.

0–87542–012–5, 336 pgs., 6 x 9, softcover   **$12.95**

IMAGICK:
THE MAGICK OF IMAGES, PATHS & DANCE
by Ted Andrews

The Qabala is rich in spiritual, mystical and magical symbols. These symbols are like physical tools, and when you learn to use them correctly, you can construct a bridge to reach the energy of other planes. The secret lies in merging the outer world with inner energies, creating a flow that augments and enhances all aspects of life.

Imagick explains effective techniques of bridging the outer and inner worlds through visualization, gesture, and dance. It is a synthesis of yoga, sacred dance and Qabalistic magick that can enhance creativity, personal power, and mental and physical fitness.

This is one of the most personal magickal books ever published, one that goes far beyond the "canned" advice other books on Pathworking give you.

0-87542-016-8, 6 x 9, 312 pgs., illus.   **$12.95**

SIMPLIFIED MAGIC
by Ted Andrews

In every person, the qualities essential for accelerating his or her growth and spiritual evolution are innate, but even those who recognize such potentials need an effective means of releasing them. The ancient and mystical Qabala is that means.

A person does not need to become a dedicated Qabalist in order to acquire benefits from the Qabala. *A reader knowing absolutely nothing about the Qabala could apply the methods in this book with noticeable success!* The Qabala is more than just some theory for ceremonial magicians. It is a system for personal attainment and magic that anyone can learn and put to use in his or her life. The secret is that the main glyph of the Qabala, the Tree of Life, is *within* you. The Tree of Life is a map to the levels of consciousness, power and magic that are within. By learning the Qabala you will be able to tap into these levels and bring peace, healing, power, love, light and magic into your life.

0-87542-015-X, 210 pgs., illus., softcover $3.95

HOW TO MAKE AND USE A MAGIC MIRROR
by Donald Tyson

There's a "boy mechanic" at home in every one of us. As Henry Ford put the world on wheels, Donald Tyson is now opening New Worlds with simple psychic technology. Author Donald Tyson takes the reader step-by-step through the creation of this powerful mystical tool. You will learn about:

- **Tools and supplies needed to create the mirror**
- **Construction techniques**
- **How to use the mirror for scrying (divination)**
- **How to communicate with spirits**
- **How to use the mirror for astral travel**

Tyson also presents a history of mirror lore in magic and literature. For anyone wanting their personal magical tool, *How to Make and Use a Magic Mirror* is a must item.

0-87542-831-2, mass market, illus. $3.95

HOW TO MAKE AN EASY CHARM TO ATTRACT LOVE INTO YOUR LIFE
by Tara Buckland

Everyone wants a happy love life. In today's world, singles organizations thrive on this fact as divorce and increased personal independence create more love-hungry people than ever. Now Tara Buckland, wife of the renowned Raymond Buckland, provides magical help for today's lonely heart.

In this book, Buckland presents:

- **An introduction to magick**
- **A quiz for the person seeking love**
- **Egyptian love spells**
- **Techniques for building an Egyptian love amulet**

All of the techniques described within are simple and non-threatening. Sometimes we all wish for a little magic in our love lives. Here's a book to fulfill our most romantic dreams.

0-87542-087-7, mass market, illus.   **$3.95**

HOW TO DREAM YOUR LUCKY LOTTO NUMBERS
by Raoul Maltagliati

Until now, there has been no scientific way to predict lotto numbers . . . they come up by chance. But overnight, you may find them through a trip into the dimension of the collective unconscious, where "time" and "chance," as we know them, do not exist.

- **Why we dream**
- **How to isolate the key points in a dream that point out your lotto numbers**
- **How to find the numberic equivalents of dream subjects**
- **How to adjust for the moon's influence on your dreams**

An extensive dream dictionary helps you discover what numbers you should pick based on your most recent dreams.

0-87542-483-X, 112 pgs., mass market   **$3.95**

THE LLEWELLYN PRACTICAL GUIDE TO ASTRAL PROJECTION.
by Denning & Phillips

Yes, your consciousness can be sent forth, out of the body, with full awareness and return with full memory. You can travel through time and space, converse with nonphysical entities, obtain knowledge by nonmaterial means, and experience higher dimensions.

Is there life after death? Are we forever shackled by time and space? The ability to go forth by means of the Astral Body, or Body of Light, gives the personal assurance of consciousness (and life) beyond the limitations of the physical body. No other answer to these ageless questions is as meaningful as experienced reality.

The reader is led through the essential stages for the inner growth and development that will culminate in fully conscious projection and return. Not only are the requisite practices set forth in step-by-step procedures, augmented with photographs and "puts-you-in-the-picture" visualization aids, but the vital reasons for undertaking them are clearly explained. Beyond this, the great benefits from the various practices themselves are demonstrated in renewed physical and emotional health, mental discipline, spiritual attainment, and the development of extra faculties.

Guidance is also given to the Astral World itself: what to expect, what can be done—including the ecstatic experience of Astral Sex between two people who project together into this higher world where true union is consummated free of the barriers of physical bodies.

0-87542-181-4, 272 pgs., 5-1/4 x 8, illus., softcover $8.95